How to Fail at Everything: A Practical Guide For

Coasting Through Life

By Lee H. Tillman

Printed in the United States of America

First Printing, 2016

Table of Contents

An Introduction to Failing

My first childhood memory is being blown in an airport bathroom in Germany. Of course my 3-year-old brain couldn't handle this many details all at once. All I knew was that I was standing in front of a giant machine that would blast me with hot air every time I pushed a button. This was of the days when a child in an airport bathroom by himself wasn't a cause for alarm. I don't know how long I was inside but eventually my older brother had to come in and get me. To this day the family joke is that I have an obsessions with hand dryers. In reality I just wanted to know how long I had to disappear before someone would come looking for me.

...

I would never recommend starting a conversation with an American Literature grad student but if you were to ask their feelings on the Robert Frost poem *The Road Not Taken* they would undoubtedly tell you how often this poem is misinterpreted. While it is often viewed as emblematic of Americas pioneering spirit, most critics see it as an example of people's tendency to look back at their accomplishments and failures and give undue credit to the decisions they made when in reality it doesn't matter. We credit a great deal of our lives to things we have no control over. For example we give a large amount of thanks to the people who raised us without fully realizing how clueless they were. In fact, I remember the exact moment I discovered that my parents were winging it and my entire family was lucky we made it out alive.

The years 1986 through 1989 were rough financial times for the Tillman household. One time my mom woke me up in the middle of the night to tell me we were leaving. She meant this literally. We were moving. For those of you that are new to the practice of "night moving" I'll explain: we were skipping out on the rent. Not long after that night I remember us living in a homeless shelter. It felt like we lived there for ages but my mom told me when I got older we had only been there for two days. Those two days were some of the most eventful days of my young life.

There was a woman who lived there whom everyone called Cain. She was visibly pregnant but she slept on her stomach. She looked like a snake that swallowed a bowling ball. One night she woke us from the fire escape outside my window singing Three Blind Mice. We moved out the next day.

One time I asked my dad when we would be moving back to our home. He replied "I don't know" and I looked back at him with a look that I didn't have the words for at 7 years old. A look that said "What the fuck! I thought you had this figured out!" He gave me a look that I'm sure all parents give when they've been caught in the headlights. A look that said, "You'll understand when you get older."

I'm now about the same age as my dad was when he told me that and I do understand what he meant. What he meant was that sometimes things don't work out the way you planned and you have to roll with the punches. The thing is I'm pretty sure I could have understood that at 7. How do I know this? **I was homeless!** Yesterday I had a bed. Today I'm sharing a cot with my little sister in a room full of schizophrenic, homeless people. When this is your life, you don't need to be 30+ to know that life is unfair.

1989 saw us "borrowing" money from my maternal grandparents so we could move back to Texas from our humble life in Virginia. We were to live in a house that my fraternal grandmother owned. It was an old house. In fact it was the house that my dad and his twin sister were born in. When it was originally built it didn't have a bathroom, just an outhouse in the backyard.

By the time we moved in the bathroom was the newest room in the house. The shower was made of unfinished, untreated wood. After a few months of use we had a bit of a mold problem. It wasn't long before there was a slimy black film covering the whole wall. My dad eventually fixed it but I don't remember anyone ever making a big deal out of the Creature from the Black Lagoon that was living on our wall. I had lived in other houses before. I knew it wasn't normal but as I had learned when I was 7 years old, life isn't always fair. So, I rolled with the punches.

This is possibly the reason why I was able to withstand nights sleeping in my car or why I stayed in relationships with people that weren't nice to me, or how I could live on $20 a week without feeling sorry for myself. I had no real fear of failure because to me failure was like a warm bath. I don't know if I could boil it all down to one experience or not. All I know is that my experiences made me just as strong as they made me weak.

...

Before we move on I should let you in on a few things about this book. Each chapter is divided into different goals in which I have failed. I tried to keep all the subjects in chronological order but sometimes things overlap or a certain topic may get ahead of itself. For instance I describe my life in high school, then college and then the workforce in that order. I also describe my nonexistent love life, which is something that has haunted me throughout all of these time periods. In order to keep from repeating information in some chapters I skimped on the details in others because talking about my love life in the Failure at Employment chapter would be irrelevant. But rest assured that everything is covered.

Also the last 2 chapters are kind of a Choose Your Own Adventure situation. Each chapter examines a different way of looking at failure. Depending on your mood or disposition you may appreciate one more than the other. If you're like me you'll read both chapters because I'm obsessed with knowing "What if?"

At any rate if for whatever reason you don't make it to the final chapter of this book that's fine. That will have mean that you've failed and therefore my book actually taught you something. Good luck.

Part I: Failing at School

When people talk to me now they usually think I must have been the perfect student. I assume this happens because I seem to know a little about a variety of subjects and my vocabulary consist of adverbs other than "really" and "super". But the truth is I was a terrible student. My classmates were always disappointed when they cheated off my paper. On my 12th grade report card I got 4 C's, 2 B's and 2 A's. The 2 A's were in Bible (yes, I took a class on the Bible in high school) and PE and they were given to me begrudgingly. My Bible teacher wrote on my report card, "Lee is a good student. He has great potential. He doesn't seem to put his all into assignments all the time." In PE I "forgot" to bring shorts once a week, which was mathematically just enough days to earn an A. Being on the Basketball and Soccer team also gave me extra points. To me school was a game that I wasn't willing to play and the few times I chose to play I surely didn't play to

win.

Chapter 1: Failing at High School

Because my older brother was getting in trouble at school my parents decided to send him to a private school. My parents liked it so much that they decided to send my sister and me there after him. It was a missionary school so there was a diverse group of White people from every continent. It was also very small even by private school standards. If two of my classmates were out sick we couldn't even play a decent hand of poker.

I learned most of what I know about politics from this school. We learned that America is a Christian country where Big Government was not to be trusted and capitalism was the answer to all the worlds' problems. We held a prayer meeting in '96 when Bill Clinton was reelected in order to prevent our nation from going to Hell. Not the euphemistic "this country is going to hell"-Hell but actual Hell. When it came to social studies we learned that Muslims wanted to kill us, people that chose to be gay were an abomination, and that Christian

Americans were becoming extinct. Speaking of extinction,
Darwin's Theory of Evolution was considered laughable and I
was never taught it my entire high school career. The school
taught kindergarten through high school. Some kids had spent
13 years of their lives taking all of this in. I only experienced
this for 4 years.

...

There is a weird theory that both Black comedians and
Fox News pundits agree on: Black people only voted for
Barack Obama because he is a Black man. The only
difference is that the comedians by definition are (kind of)
joking. I disagree with this idea completely. Not just because
it's offensive to suggest that Black people only care about race
and we're not smart enough to form an intelligent opinion but
because this idea has been proven wrong quite a few times: In
2016 with Ben Carson, in 2012 with Herman Cain and in 1996,
2000 and 2008 with Alan Keys. Not even Shirley Chisholm '72,
Jesses Jackson '84, '88 and Al Sharpton '04 could motivate us

although that may have had more to do with the times in which they ran.

The person on this list that is nearest and dearest to my heart is Alan Keys. Not because I would have voted for him in 1996 if I were old enough but because this was the first time anyone ever asked me about a political candidate. It's pretty clear now that everyone at my school was planning on voting for Bob Dole but everyone always asked me what I thought about Alan Keys. They assumed that I, like him, was a Black Republican and I would have some special insight.

What they didn't know was that I wasn't a Republican. Nor was I a Democrat. I was 16. I had no idea what any of this even meant. I gave speeches about personal accountability over giving handouts, the illegality of abortions, and the persecution of Christians by not allowing prayer in schools but I was just parroting the bullet points given to me. They saw me as "one of the good ones." Or as Ann Coulter once said "Our [meaning Republicans] blacks are so much better than their [meaning Democrats] blacks". Up until I graduated the only politics I had ever been exposed to where right wing politics. And it wasn't until I examined the rest of the world that I realize that I had been playing for the wrong team.

Although I disagree with 90% of what I was taught it was still a valuable experience. True, public schools did teach me evolution but they barely taught me how to read. When I got to private school I was a terrible speller. I was so bad that in my junior year of high school I had to take an orthography (spelling) class. Most of the kids in the class weren't even in high school. Going to this class reminded me of when I was in sixth grade and my homeroom was in the Special Education building. I don't know if it was a paperwork mix-up or if the school really thought I was mentally challenged.

But unlike the Special Education debacle I undoubtedly belonged in Orthography. I frustrated my teachers when I read out loud. They tried to be patient but it defiantly wore on them. Although it made me a better speller I'm still too ashamed to spell anything out loud. For me, spelling in public is like taking first year Spanish and them moving to Argentina. More often than not I'll spell the word correctly but I don't trust myself enough to know the answer. I've lost friends for not coming to their game night out of fear they would make me play Scrabble.

While Orthography did help me I had the same problems I always had in school: I didn't see the point in any of it. It didn't help that I was taking classes such as Latin, Bible and Logic. At my school the only electives were sports. (It just hit me how ironic it was that I took Logic at this school.) We also took Sentence Analysis, which doesn't sound that bad until you realize that we had to take the same class every year.

What class I took didn't actually matter because I did the least amount of work I possibly could in all of them. I feel like my teachers passed me because they didn't want to deal with me. In my mind an A didn't move me on to the next grade any faster so why not settle for a C.

One thing the more intimate private school setting helped me deal with was my introversion. The classes were so small I had no choice but to become close with the kids around me. I had the same teenage insecurities as anyone else but those insecurities are much easier to deal with when you're not afraid of being beat up for wearing the wrong colors. The people there were always friendly but I was never sure that we were friends. There were certainly days when I felt like a friend but many others where I felt like a mascot.

...

For some reason in the late nineties the Afro made a comeback. Every guy I saw on the street hade one, every guy at my church grew one, and even Ice Cube sported one. I felt it was time for me. I never minded if the kids at my school wanted to touch my hair as long as they asked first. I'm sure my hair got touched without me knowing a few times. After a while it was time for family pictures and my mom was not having my afrocentricities ruining her picture. I reluctantly shaved it off.

The next day I came to school late. I don't remember why. I walked in with a hoodie covering my head and sat down. Everyone could tell I had cut my hair but no one said a word. My teacher made me leave to get a late pass from the principal's office and right before I walked out the door I flipped my hood off to reveal my shorn head. As they saw my head everyone began to cheer. To this day I still don't completely understand their reaction. Where they cheering the sheer excitement of me getting a drastic haircut or did they just really not like my hair? I never got an answer for that one. Things like this often left me baffled but they were mostly harmless. Every now and then things got a little tougher to deal with.

Once in my American Literature class we were asked to choose an author on which to write a report. My teacher went around the room asking whom we wanted to write about and he wrote are choices in his textbook. I naturally chose Langston Hughes. He wrote down my name and finished his lesson. A couple of hours later I had another class in the same room and my best friend and I saw his textbook lying on the windowsill. We picked it up hoping to see some answers for next weeks quiz. What we found was much more informative.

My friend turned to the page with the list of authors with our names beside it and his face immediately fell. He pointed to the page and looked up at me without saying a word. Scribbled next to the name Langston Hughes in my teachers' handwriting read the phase "black kid". My heart sank.

Keep in mind that this teacher, who was also the headmaster of the school, had known my family and me for about four years. The class we were in was a combination of the sophomore and junior class, which came to about 12 students. To his credit it wasn't just *my* name that he forgot. He put "adopted kid" beside the kid that sat a few seats behind me. What hurt me wasn't that he had forgotten my name. It was that to him after my name my only defining factor was my race. For some reason I thought we were past that phase in our relationship.

A few periods later I had him for yet another class and I sat patiently hoping that he would call on me. When he finally did I pounced.

"So, you know my name now?"

"Of course I do. I've known your family for years."

"Then why didn't you write that in your book."

"What?"

"In your book it says 'black kid'."

"..."

I could see in his eyes that he knew exactly what I was talking about. The class sat in an understandably uncomfortable silence for a few moments before erupting into laughter. I had caught the teacher with his pants down. Score one for the students, right?

I sat in silence awaiting my answer. After stammering for a few seconds he finally admitted that he had just forgotten my name and couldn't think of anything else to write. He eventually got the class to settle down and he continued with the lesson. After class I went up to him and confronted him again. His only response was "Were you trying to embarrass me?" He sounded hurt as if I had betrayed his trust. I don't remember if he every apologized or if he really knew what I was upset about. I do remember that we never talked about it again.

Maybe I *was* asking too much of him. As a kid you're taught that we're all just people and that if you just keep assimilating one day you're race won't matter. At least that's what minority kids are taught. I'm pretty sure the thought of assimilation never occurs to White American kids. What would they assimilate to?

I can't say my life would have gotten better or worse had I stayed in public school but I can say without equivocation that I dodged a bullet by not being homeschooled. For about 3 days in my senior year this was a reality. Luckily 2 of those days were the weekend.

One month my parents couldn't pay tuition and instead of working on a payment plan with the school they decided to homeschool my sister and me. The idea probably came from the fact that my mom worked at a Christian bookstore. How she saw the homeschooled kids and thought that that would be the perfect life for my sister and me I do not know.

I don't remember actually doing anything the day that we didn't go to school. I only remember the end of the day when my mom told us that my grandparents agreed to pay the tuition they owed and that we would be going back to school.

The headmaster at my school was baffled that my parents didn't come and talk to him first about their payment. I'll admit I was a bit baffled too. It can't be legal to just pull your kid out of school in the middle of the semester and start homeschooling them. Isn't there paperwork to fill out? Doesn't the government need to be alerted? Don't you have to at least tell the school you're not coming back? Both my parents worked. Who was going to stay at home and homeschool us? It was all incredibly baffling.

I completely understand them not wanting to ask their parents for assistance though. My grandfather would never let them forget it. On top of that my grandmother was a public school teacher. She couldn't be happy about her daughter choosing homeschooling over public school. To be honest I don't understand how anyone could choose homeschooling over anything. I've seen research that suggests that homeschooled kids are no less social adjusted than public schooled kids. I've also met a few homeschooled kids and I can't believe any of that is true. I don't understand how a high school aged kids spending 7-8 hours a day with their mother doesn't drive them to grow up to be a serial killer. Clearly I'm wrong because most serial killers go to public school.

...

It's hard for me to tell how much of the homophobia I witnessed at school was due to religion or the times I grew up in. Whether you are for or against gay marriage, if you were a teenager any time in American history before 2010 you have to be stunned at the strides the movement has made in the few short years after. Before 2010 no matter what god you worshiped "No Homo" was a pretty ubiquitous phrase and sitting next to another dude in a movie theater was a transgression punishable by death. Still, the fact that our school philosophy was that homosexuals should literally be burned in a lake of fire would lead me to believe that it was probably more about religion than the fact that it was the 90s.

Our South African gym teacher thought it was weird that we didn't shower after class but he never made us. He also tried to teach us how to play rugby but it soon fell apart when he tried to describe to us what a "scrum" was. In case you've never seen one it is basically a play in which each team gets into a group hug and challenges the other team for the ball by butting head like a couple of rams trying to impress their mates. No one in my class was comfortable with this arrangement. Yet putting your hands between another mans legs for him to hand you a ball was somehow acceptable.

After games if someone wanted to shower we did it one by one or in the sink. When we had overnight trips guys would sleep on the floor rather than be in bed next to their classmates. I can't honestly say that I was innocent to everything that went on. While I never actively participated in any of this I never condemned it either. Even if I had I'm not sure what I would have said.

"Stop squirming when you think about a man speaking with a lisp."

"Seeing the crack of my ass in the shower won't make you gay."

"You don't have to sleep fully covered on top of the sheets."

Maybe I could have said that but I was a teenager who just wanted to fit in. When you're 16 conformity trumps civil duty every time. The one thing I learned from my time there was that homophobia is really inconvenient and unnecessarily sweaty.

...

One day when I came to school one of my classmates wanted to have a talk with me about something she saw at a friend's house that deeply disturbed her. It was a picture of "Black Jesus" or as some people call him "Jesus". She couldn't make heads or tails of it. Clearly Jesus wasn't Black but was she racist for believing that? Would I be offended if she thought the idea of a Black Jesus was preposterous? When she brought it up I didn't know what to tell her and I still don't. I don't know if Jesus was Black or not but it's pretty obvious that Michelangelo and da Vinci's version of him looks nothing like a Middle Eastern Jew.

To me the question is never "What did Jesus look like?" the question is "Why was it so easy to convince people he looked like that?" The most quoted description of Jesus is in Revelations 1:14. It says that his hair was white as wool and his feet were like bronze. It also says that his eyes were like fire, in his hand he held seven stars and a double-edged sword was coming out of his mouth. I'm not sure how literally we should be taking all of this. In all honesty most of the Book of Revelations sounds like John the Apostle was on an acid trip.

Even if we do take it literally the idea of Jesus being blonde-haired and blue-eyed is pretty universal and looks nothing like it says in Revelations. Jesus looks like that because that's what we wanted him to look like. We wanted him to look like that because there was no way white Catholics and Protestants were going to deify a guy that looked like a Middle Eastern Jew.

One argument is that His race doesn't matter. If He rescued you from eternal damnation it doesn't matter if He was lily white or pitch black. This argument is well and good but the only time I ever hear anyone say, "it doesn't matter what color Jesus is" is when He's being accused of being non-White.

To assuage my classmates' fear I let her know that I didn't think any less of her and that we were still friends. People see god in different ways and this was one of them. Black Jesus is not a different god than Jesus. You may continue worshiping your white god if you like. No conversion is needed. However you would be more accurate in your worship if you did.

...

On our soccer team there was an Indian kid named Ajit who was nice but a little too nebbish at times. Once before a match I saw him staring at the opposing team with complete terror in his eyes and I had the pleasure of overhearing the following conversation:

My teammate Phil: "What's wrong?"

Ajit: "That guy over there."

Phil: "Which one."

Ajit: "The one with the specks. He looks tough. I can't guard him."

Phil: "Which one? They're all Spics."

Ajit: "No, 'specks'. Glasses."

There's so much going on in this conversation that it's hard to suss out the most surprising element. Did Phil think that Ajit, a kid who had moved to the states only months ago, would know what the word 'Spic' means in America? Did Phil think 'Spic' was a term used worldwide? Did he think that India has an equally tumultuous relationship with Latin America as the US? When he though Ajit said 'Spic' why did he continue the conversation with no hesitation? Did he think it was OK to use a pejorative term for an ethnic group as long as no one from that ethnic group was around? Ok this one I probably know the answer to. I was probably most surprised because I had never heard Phil talk that way before. The conversations we had in class about immigration took on a more sinister tone after hearing this.

...

I spent all four of my high school years just trying to make it to the next grade. By the time I was a senior I had run out of grades and in effect had run out of goals. My classmates' goals where typically to either join a missionary team and travel the world spreading the word of god, marry the person to their left and have half a dozen kids or both. Not only did none of those things interest me they didn't even feel like options. Only someone who had received the pre-K to high school level of "training" would consider being a missionary a job and being the only person of color didn't do me any favors in the dating department. I felt like I left high school like an inmate leaves prison: with the clothes on my back and just enough to get me a few miles up the road.

Come to think of it, that's probably how most people leave

high school.

Chapter 2: Failing at College Part I

I always envied people that knew what they wanted to be since they were young. It seems that every artists' bio involves an infant picking up a guitar and teaching itself how to play. As a kid I never knew what I wanted to be. No one around me was doing anything particularly interesting so my idea of being a grown-up was waking up, going to work at a job you only tolerate because it pays you, coming home, and going to sleep so that you could wake up the next morning and do it again.

In elementary school when I was asked what I wanted to be I said "truck driver", not because I wanted to be one but because that was what the kid before me said. The only thing I was truly passionate about was music but I had no real desire to be an artist. At least no more that any other person my age that grew up watching MTV. When I was 15 I saw an ad in the back of a magazine promoting a school for recording arts. I figured that was probably my best shot at getting in the music industry without being an artist. This was the first time I ever thought about my future seriously and I didn't think about it again until the day before I graduated from high school.

I had no real plans after high school other than to go to the junior college in my city. My parents couldn't tell me much about college because they had never been. My dad was drafted into the Army out of high school and my mother followed him. My parents never had professional jobs. They just moved through life the best they could, as I'm sure is the process of most working class families; just keep your head down and hope for the best.

My time at Tyler Junior College was just as unfocused as the rest of my life had been. On my college entrance exam my writing score was fine but my math score was abysmal. So much so that I had to take the first level of remedial math before I could actually take any college level math courses. I did well enough in the first level that the next semester I was able to take level 3 remedial math. Unfortunately I failed level 3 and had to repeat it in the summer.

Before my last semester at junior college I went to see an academic counselor to see what I had to do to get a degree. He looked at my transcript, tried not to laugh, suggested a few courses and shortly thereafter I was awarded an Associated Degree in Interdisciplinary Studies. Sometimes I forget I have this degree. I eventually stopped putting it on my resume.

After 2 years At Tyler Junior College I transferred to Prairie View A& M University, a historically Black University (HBU) just outside of Houston. I only applied to one school and I only applied to the school because my cousin Renaldo had recently graduated from there. Everyone around me said it was a good move so I went along. I honestly don't even remember applying. Like most people that didn't know anything about going to college I majored in Communications. My older cousin had enough sense to major in Engineering. Since I went to Prairie View A&M a few of my younger cousins have followed suit but as far as I know Renaldo was the only one to make his journey worthwhile.

I hardly remember anything about my academic life other than I had a professor that told me I should write for the school paper. She was the first and the last person to ever tell me I was good at something. People throughout my life told me I was smart but no one had ever told me I was actually good at anything. It's also possible that she just needed someone to join the school newspaper so that it didn't shut down from lack of interest. She was 30 years old with a PhD and pretty in a Phylicia Rashad in the 80s sort of way so naturally I did whatever she told me. I spent most of my time on the paper writing music reviews.

One of the only assignments I remember having while a communications major had to do with creating an episode of a TV show that we created ourselves. We were separated into groups and each group had to designate a writing team, an engineering team, a director, and select the on-air talent. I hated and still hate group assignments. My success depending on someone else's competence has always felt Un-American to me.

I believe that group assignments are in theory a good idea but are completely useless in practice. Theoretically, working with your classmates should teach you how to deal with your coworkers in the real world. The only difference being that in the real world the people you work with were picked for their specific strengths. Someone felt that your coworker was competent enough to handle what was being asked of him or her but more importantly your coworker could be fired if he or she didn't pull his or her weight.

Group assignments are like standing at a crowded intersection waiting for the walk light and then challenging the crowd on the other side of the street to a game of basketball. Sure some of the people on my corner are up for the task but I don't think the pregnant woman pushing the stroller is going to be able to d-up the way I need her to. Put it this way: group assignments are so disastrous that they are the basis for literally every reality TV game show ever made.

To make matters worse my group consisted of people that couldn't get into the other groups. If any of us were lucky enough to have friends none of them took this class. In other words we were the leftovers and the fact that we weren't assertive enough to interject ourselves into a group made for lousy leadership. In fact it was so lousy that I was designated as the leader.

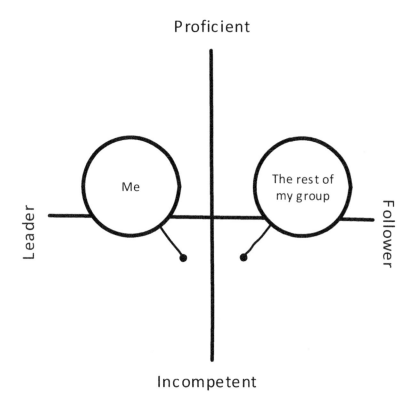

Our group meetings were consistently canceled. When we did get around to meeting they never seemed to lead anywhere. Before we knew it our presentation date was staring us in the face. Like a good leader I told everyone not to worry. I would come up with something.

I think our professor wanted all of us to create a news program but the group that went before us chose to go in a different direction: Daytime Talk Show. Think Jerry Springer meets… well it was Jerry Springer. It was funny and well directed and our professor loved it. My idea was for our group to do the exact same thing. To my credit I asked the other group leader for permission before completely ripping her off. She asked me if I had any other ideas. I said "no". She replied, "I guess it's OK. I already got my grade. Besides, what else are you going to do? You only have 5 days." My sentiments exactly.

I spent the next five days writing the script, deciding on camera angles, and picking the music cues. When I brought it to my group they all agreed without hesitation because like someone else had already pointed out "what else were we going to do."

Five days later I watched as my show fell flat on its face. I felt like a network executive that tried to adapt a popular British TV series for an American audience after only seeing one episode. The acting was stiff because the actors had almost no time to learn their lines, none of the jokes were landing because I wrote them without asking for anyone's input, and I really didn't know what I was doing in the control booth. The music cues were pretty good though.

The worst part about it was that this was all on me. I was the one who made all this happen. I was the one who wasted everyone's time. I was the one who failed my team.

My only solace was that I taught everyone what *not* to do. I don't remember what grade we got but my professor did make a decree that there would be no more comedic talk shows. For the rest of the semester I went on being ignored by my classmates and was only mentioned when in comparison to other shoddy works. I overheard "At least it's better than Lee's" mentioned more times than I'd like to remember. After that semester I changed my focus to the lucrative world of print journalism and never looked back.

...

I wasn't in college long before things got out of hand. By "out of hand" I wish I meant drugs, women and alcohol but sadly I'm referring to my financial status. I had taken too long to get a job and when I finally did I was already in the hole. I had a $400 car note because I had missed few payments, a $160 insurance payment again because I missed a few payments, a ¼ tank of gas, a 20-mile drive to work and $12 to my name. I was also about to get kicked out of my apartment for failing to pay rent. I tried asking my parents for help but they had their own money problems so I had to follow the family tradition of asking my grandparents. I came to this realization while I was standing on a street corner, begging strangers for gas money. Keep in mind that this was of the days when gas was $1.50 a gallon.

I hated asking my grandparents for money because in a town where everyone leased brand new cars and parked them next to dilapidated houses, my grandfather was easily the most independent person I knew. He owned the house he lived in and he had his own business. In my lifetime I had never seen my grandfather answer to anyone other than his customers and in his seventies he was still the hardest working man I had ever known. Me asking him and my grandmother for money felt like I was letting them down and even worst following in the footsteps of everyone else in the family including my own parents. Another reason why I wasn't looking forward to this was because my grandfather wasn't the kind of man to let things like this go by without reminding me of how he saved me from financial ruin every time I saw him. I would be hearing about this until the day I paid him back or until I was on my deathbed because he would certainly outlive me. I also saw what a life of being in debt to other people did to my parents. It always seemed like everything they owned could be taken away at anytime. It took me years to realize that everything could be taken away from you no matter how financially stable you are.

This was the first time my grandparents directly bailed me out and sadly it wasn't the last. My grandparents lent me the money and I was officially put on the books. Of course this didn't solve everything but it was a start, a very small start.

The job that I got while I was at college was at the Wal-Mart 20 miles away from where I lived. More ambitious students had taken all of the jobs that were closer to me. Before I left for work one day I saw that my tank was dangerously close to empty so I said a prayer to the same god that fed the multitudes with a fish and a loaf to provide me safe passage. Naturally, I ran out of gas.

Running out of gas if your gage is broken or if you're just not paying attention is regrettable. But running out of gas because you don't have the money is demoralizing. It's the grownup version of watching your ice cream fall to the floor only less terrifying. I hitchhiked and made it to work only 10 minutes late.

I was scheduled to work from 3 pm until 12 am. No one was going home the way I did so I couldn't ask for a ride. I also didn't know anyone well enough to crash on their couch. To make matters worse I had to be at work at 10 o'clock the next morning. Lucky for me just outside the entrance of the store, Wal-Mart was having a sale on canopied porch swings so I wrapped my jacket around me, pushed the swings close together so none could see me, and spent the night under the stars. Two thoughts crossed my mind as the wind violently blew my canopy swing back and forth all night: 1) What I was going to say if someone saw me and 2) what was I doing with my life?

I awoke the next morning and got breakfast off the dollar menu at McDonalds. After I ate I snuck into the store because I didn't want anyone who worked overnight to see me. I bought a travel-sized mouthwash, deodorant and a black T-shirt because I didn't want anyone to see me in the same clothes. Including breakfast this all cost me about $7, which was half of the money I had left in the world. I took a nap in the break room, and mulled around the store for a bit before I clocked in. Either no one noticed or no one cared, probably both. Sadly this wasn't the last time I ran out of money for gas but when it happened the next time I had a plan: I stole money out of the register.

Before I tell you about the next time I was stranded I'll tell you about the day before. It was my 21st birthday and I was working late. The combination of having parents with drinking problems and growing up in a dry county left me inexperienced when it came to booze. I only say that to explain why I bought a six-pack of Smirnoff Ice. Only the cashier that checked me out knew it was my birthday. I got home, made dinner, drank and fell asleep watching TV.

The next day was New Years Eve and I had to work late again. On the way back home my car broke down about 5 miles after I passed the only gas station on the highway. I walked back along the side of the highway in the cold to get some help. At the gas station I saw a cop who when I asked for help informed me that he "wasn't a taxi service." Fair enough.

The clerk told me that there was a young guy outside that

was in the same predicament and he was waiting for his father-in-law to pick him up and drive him to Houston. I asked him if he could help me and he wasn't sure if his father-in-law would agree but he said that I could ask. He would have called him and asked but his father-in-law had already left the house and cell phones weren't as ubiquitous as they are now.

After I got in his car we mutually agreed that awkward silence was the way we were going to handle the situation. When the ball dropped I was freezing my butt off in a drafty Mustang with a complete stranger hoping that I could get a ride home. An hour later his father-in-law showed up and he agreed to give me a ride. When I got home I took a shower and passed out on the couch. I wonder if that guy, wherever he is, ever thinks about the New Years Eve he gave a random dude a ride home.

My last attempt at normalcy before dropping out of college was trying to pledge a fraternity. Seeing as I was attending a Historically Black University there were only five choices: Phi Beta Sigma, Iota Phi Theta, Kappa Alpha Psi,

Omega Psi Phi, and Alpha Phi Alpha. At my school Phi Beta Sigma and Iota Phi Theta were the frats you pledged if you couldn't into any others. Kappa Alpha Psi were the pretty boys and Omega Psi Phi were practically a street gang. I chose Alpha Phi Alpha. (Full disclosure: my oldest brother is Alpha Phi Alpha.)

There was a guy in my class who was an Alpha so I asked him what I needed to do. He told me to meet him in his dorm room that evening and bring money. I don't remember how much he asked for but any amount he asked for would have been all I had. When I showed up his room was lit with candles. I don't know if this was to invoke mystery, if he was trying to seduce me, or if he just really liked candles. Regardless, I acted as if there was noting weird about this and gave him the reverence I thought he deserved.

I remember he had an AΦA throw rug on his floor and I circumvented it out of respect. After noticing my awkwardness he told me it was OK to walk on it. He then asked me why I wanted to pledge. I gave him the typical job interview answers and he seemed impressed. The first step was for me to memorize the seven jewels (founding fathers) of Alpha Phi Alpha. He said he could help me get in if I was serious and I assured him I was. I only went back one more times.

This wasn't because I wasn't serious, or because I was scared or because I was running out of money (although all of those things played factors), it was because sometime after that second encounter I had my first panic attack. I couldn't go outside without feeling as though my heart would burst from my chest. This combined with my debilitating depression prevented me from going to class anymore.

It's hard to describe what a panic attack feels like. The best description I can think of is imagining how you would feel if you saw a bear charging toward you. Now take away the bear. That's what a panic attack feels like. You remember what triggered the panic attack last time and you fear that if you walk into a crowded room, or get in your car, or get asked a certain question you may have another panic attack. Pretty soon the idea of having a panic attack scares you so much that you have a panic attack.

Depression on the other hand feels completely different. It's like eating your favorite meal and then loosing your sense of taste halfway through. You feel completely numb but also terrified that this numbness is all you'll ever feel again. So during this time I was oscillating between fear and numbness on an hourly basis.

I spent the next few months either in my apartment crying or at work trying no to. When I wasn't crying I was sleep. Not necessarily because I was tired but because I didn't want to be awake. Like Joey Ramone I wanted to be sedated but I didn't have any money for drugs or alcohol. Sleeping all day was the most cost effective solution. Although sleeping while I was supposed to be in class only wasted the money I spent on college so I guess the joke was on me.

Even though I had dealt with depression since I was a teenager this was the first time I had actually felt suicidal. I remember one day while driving to work I thought about swerving off the road and I immediately began crying. I cried because I couldn't believe that things had gotten to this point. The only thing that prevented me from doing it was knowing that with my luck it probably wouldn't work. I would just end up with a totaled car and a broken arm I couldn't explain. I pulled over and cried for about ten minutes. I made it a mile from work before it started all over again. I sat in the parking lot and balled my eyes out for 15 minutes before I could walk in. I ended up being late for work because I couldn't figure out what I was supposed to be doing with my life.

This part of my life is the hardest to look back on because it's hard to believe that it was me. I still get frustrated with my life sometimes and I wonder if it would just be better if I burned everything to the ground. But I never feel like ending it. I still cry but it's never out of desperation. And I still get panic attacks. The last memorable one I had was while I was jogging. It was very confusing to not know if your heart was beating fast because you are running in a circle or because *you are running in a circle.* But the attacks are so infrequent that they're more surprising than scary.

The hardest part for me to understand is how I got through it. I wouldn't call what I went though "rock bottom" but it was far from a bad case of the weepies. I think what happened was that I realized that I wasn't going to kill myself. Then I woke up one morning and said, "OK, if you're not going to kill yourself, what are you going to do?" That was it.

...

As a grad student years later I received a letter to join my schools chapter of Alpha Phi Alpha. I took it as a sign and attended an informational meeting. Everyone who was pledging was significantly younger than me. It also seemed like the older members and the younger members where in the midst of a standoff. Nothing felt right. By that time in my life I was too comfortable with myself to let them tell me that I needed them. Had they caught me before the panic attacks I probably would have pledged but they were too late.

...

Me dropping out of school was more out of necessity than choice. I hadn't been to class for months so finals were out of the question. The thought of moving back to Tyler, TX and living with my parents again never occurred to me. That was when I thought about the ad I saw in the back of a magazine when I was 15. I decided I was going to move to Orlando, FL to learn to be a recording engineer.

I wrote my parents a letter telling them about my breakdown. I assured them I was OK and that I was moving to Florida. This was the hardest thing I had ever had to tell them. Until then the hardest thing I ever had to tell them was that I wasn't going to church. I felt like I had let everyone down but the stronger feeling I had was needing to make a decision that was mine and mine alone. I didn't go back to visit them before I left so there was no real way for anyone to talk me out of it.

The first time I ever got drunk in my life was at my going away party. The only experience I took away from being drunk is that when I have children, I'm going to teach them how to drink. No one ever tells you that you don't have to drink like

John Belushi in Animal House (or Will Ferrel in Old School or

insert current popular comedian in *insert current popular*

college film). No one ever tells you that when you drink the

hangover and vomiting is completely optional. I walked around

the party swilling a bottle of cheap whiskey and fell asleep on

the nearest couch. The next morning I felt fine. I drove myself

home and finished packing for my 12-hour drive to Orlando,

FL. On my way to put the first box in the car I got a massive

headache and realized that I didn't eat anything the night

before. I knew that you shouldn't drink on an empty stomach

but I didn't have any money for food and the booze was free. I

spent the next 30 minutes dry heaving in my empty apartment.

After lying on my back for about an hour with the room

spinning I finally felt well enough to start my journey. I finished

packing up my car and never looked back.

Chapter 3: Failing at College Part II

When I finally got to Orlando I pulled out my map (yes, I owned a physical map) and tried to find my new apartment. By the time I found the place it was dusk and because I didn't have the keys and I didn't have any money I pulled into the complex in front of my new home and slept in my car until morning. I discovered after I awoke the next morning that the apartment was unlocked and I immediately started moving in.

At this point in my life I had never leased a place on my own and didn't know that you had to sign a lease before it was officially yours. My new landlord was not happy and luckily she didn't kick me out. After I finished signing everything I decided to take a tour of the school campus seeing as it was only a few miles away. On the way back I pulled into a drive though restaurant called Krystal. It's basically the South's version of White Castle. I only mention this fact for 2 reasons: 1) I was flat broke and under no other circumstances would I eat there and 2) for reasons that will be evident in a moment this place is forever etched in my mind.

After coming back from seeing my new school I was excited for the future and wondering if I could realty make this work. This was the furthest I had ever been from home without the intent of retuning. I was in a new city and completely alone. As I took a right turn into the parking lot of Krystal I heard a terrifying scrap and my car shook like I had just run over something. I looked into the rearview mirror and saw my driver side rear wheel rolling out into the street where it wobbled like a freshly spun coin before it toppled over.

I want to make this clear; when I say "wheel" I don't mean the tire or the hubcap. I mean the wheel, the tire, and the rim: all gone. Luckily there where no cars in the street so aside from my pride, hopes, and pocketbook nothing and no one was hurt. I walked to the payphone (yes, payphone) called a tow truck, ordered a Krystal Chik, sat on the corner and waited. I called my grandmother to see if she could wire me some money to pay the driver to haul the car away because I knew it couldn't be fixed. I don't remember if she sent the money but I do remember walking home and wondering if I was really going to be able to do this. It would be 6 years before I would own a car again.

When I got to Florida I had to wait for my checks from my two previous jobs for about a couple of weeks. I literally had no money for the first five days I was there. Eventually I received my check from one place but not from the other. I forgot to tell them my apartment number so it got returned and they had to send it again. I had to call my grandmother and ask her for $50 to cover me for a few days. It took 2 months to finally get my second check.

I forgot to mention that while I was in Prairie View A & M I self published my first book. It was during these first few months in Orlando that I received my first royalty check. It was for $50. It would also be the last royalty check I ever received from that book.

...

In Orlando I was attending a private art school that taught videogame, film, music production and recording. Nerds of all types were represented. Our first day of class was orientation. We all met for what I guess could be called an assembly and we heard all of our future professors give speeches about what we would learn in their respective classes. The last speaker was what in a normal school you would call the Dean or the President but I think the best title for him would have been Owner. He gave a speech about how we had all come from far off places to start our new lives. How we weren't like other students that went off to "traditional" universities. We were special. We had a calling. At the end of his speech I, like many of my classmates, shed a tear because we did feel special. We had tumultuous journeys and now we had finally arrived. This was the start of a new chapter in our lives. That was also the only time I ever saw my school president/owner. The emotional intensity also kind of wore off when I realized that this speech was repeated every month when new students were admitted.

I took my classes seriously. I was there for audio recording but in the beginning we had to take classes from all the disciplines. I took classes in film production, computer animation, live recording and a host of others that I can't remember. The most important thing I remember from those classes is how beautiful it was to see people in their element. There were people there that couldn't make direct contact with strangers but if they were put in front of a computer screen they became Fred Astaire.

The school was open 24 hours. We were told that this was because in the industry we would be working at all hours of the night and we needed to adjust to having a recording session at 4am. My natural cynicism partly believed this was done so that they could accommodate more students and therefor get more money. There was probably truth to both of those statements.

I bought a bike so I could get back and forth from school. I got the money from working on campus as a tour guide and a "student ambassador". These were typical jobs for most of the students there. We would call prospective students and talk to them about the school. Most of the time it was OK with the exception of a few upset parents that wanted their son or daughter to go to a "real" school. It was understandable.

I wasn't making much money working for the school so most of my money was coming from my student loan. Unfortunately it was taking longer than expected for the funds to appear. Within a few months of living in my new apartment I couldn't pay my rent. I also discovered that when I moved into my apartment my electricity bill was never changed over into my name. The bills were going to the complex instead of me. My complex never bothered to tell me this until 3 days before they were about to disconnect my electricity. It was Friday and my bank wasn't open on the weekend so even if I did scrape up the money I would be cutting it pretty close. It was almost the first so on top of owing rent I also owed her money for two months of electricity.

I called my landlord to let her know my situation and she proceeded to yell at me for what felt like hours. I'm pretty sure that was the day that I realized that I was an adult. Initially I thought it was the day that I picked out my own cereal at the grocery store but I was mistaken. Because my landlord didn't believe me I asked my financial advisor at the school to give her a call and explain the situation. My landlord yelled at my financial advisor just the same. I called my grandmother to see if she could help me. My landlord didn't yell at her. She just hung up on my grandmother, twice.

It was now the first and I was trembling all the way to the managers' office with my rent check trying to figure out what to say when she asked me about my electric bill. Luckily no one was in the office because they were remodeling and I was spared the humiliation. I left the money in the drop box and scurried away.

Afterwards I called a girl I went to college with in Texas to whom I was in unrequited love with to fill her in on my sad story and she told me in so many words that I was too emotionally draining and she didn't want to talk to me anymore. I scrapped together the few dollars I had and went grocery shopping just so I could have the distinct experience of having someone being pleasant to me. When the automatic doors slid open and the woman at the counter greeted me I looked her in her eyes and thanked her with every molecule in my body.

Because my electricity was eventually turned off I had to temporarily move in with a friend who lived a few blocks away. At the ripe old age of 21 he and I were the elder statesmen of our class of 19 year olds. This was evident when the cops raided a party at his apartment complex and everyone ran but us.

We recorded songs, watched movies, drank beer, and even made Thanksgiving Dinner together. As much as I loved having a friend to hang out with all the time there was nothing like having my own place. After a month my financial aid check finally came and I was able to turn my lights back on and move back to my old place. After that everything else picked up. It was hard to believe at the time but looking back this was probably the most carefree I had ever been.

In school I learned how to record on some of the most expensive and high tech sound boards at the time. I learned how to properly mic a drum kit and how to use a soldering iron but my favorite class was music history. I even stayed late so I could let my professor know how much his class meant to me. He replied, "Really, you might want to rethink that?" I should have taken that as a sign but of course I didn't.

For the first 11 months of my 12 month program I was on fire and for the first time in my school career I was a strait A student. Near the end I spent most of my free time looking for internships in cities all over America. In 2002 there was a resurgence of Philadelphia music (The Roots, Jaguar Wright,

Jill Scott, Jazzy Jeff, Bilal, etc.) and I wanted in. Of the dozens of studios I applied for I only heard back from 3 or 4. One studio even told me that this was the wrong time to be a recording engineer and that I especially shouldn't move to a new city to pursue it. I also should have taken that as a sign but of course I didn't.

The only positive emails I received were from studios in Los Angeles. One was in Studio City and the other was in Hollywood. One weekend I flew out for interviews. I particularly remember these flights because they were my first flights after 9/11. The first time I had to take off my shoes in an airport. I also remember this flight because it was the first flight I had taken as an adult. Every other time I had flown someone else paid for my seat and made sure I arrived on time. This was the first time in my life I was in charge of all of this and there were a few little things I didn't know how to handle. For instance since my flight from Orlando to Los Angels was over 3 hours and I didn't know that a meal was included in my plane ticket.

When the flight attendant came around with everyone's food I decided to pass because I didn't have the money to pay for a fancy airplane meal. The flight attendant looked perplexed when I turned it down. The lady next to me asked if I was sure. I stood firm. I was not about to get suckered. I starved myself throughout the entire 6-hour plane trip. I did not, however, turn down the hot towel though I did not know what to do with it.

I was so enamored with Los Angeles that I hardly remember the interviews. Although it might have been possible that I was just so hungry when I got off the plane. I remember getting on a city bus and thinking almost out loud, "Wow, all these people are Los Angelinos." All I remember about my meetings is that the place in Studio City didn't seem too impressed and the one in Hollywood said to give them a call when I moved to LA. That settled it. I was moving to LA.

In my last month of school I came down with a near fatal case of Senioritis. I skipped classes and fell asleep in lectures. For one class I even stole a copy of the test but I still failed because I was too lazy to study the answers. One of my last finals was hands-on. The professor left me in the recording studio all by myself for 20 minutes and all I had to do was get sound to come out of the monitors by way of an SSL mixing board. After my 20 minutes was up the professor returned to find me practically in tears. He was flabbergasted. If I couldn't do this what the Hell had I been doing for the past year?

I failed my final with what I'm assuming was a 0, which meant that I failed my last class with a 66 and those 4 points made sure that I would not graduate. I had a choice to make: Leave for LA and start at the recording studio in October like I promised or stay in Orlando another month and get the degree for which I had sacrificed a year of my life. I went home, packed my things and procured a 12-foot Penske moving truck going one way. I was officially dropping out of college for a second time.

Part II: Failing at Artistry

I always felt weird calling myself an artist. In fact I still don't call myself an artist. Art is something that is done by people with special gifts. I never felt like anything I did was particularly special. Anyone could write poetry, or write a story. There's no certification you need to get to tell a joke or record a song. If Shawn Brown AKA the Rappin' Duke could make a rap song...

My biggest problem with me wanting to become an artist was the word that almost always precedes it: "starving". The practical side of me had no desire to go down that road but the truth is I really like creating art. I mean look at me: I wrote a book when literally no one asked me to. The idea that I could be recognized for something that came out of my brain is the only real driving force I've had since I was 7. The problem was I wasn't really good at anything. At least I didn't think I was.

The city of Los Angeles is included in this section as a separate entity because aside from New York there is no other city in America that has so many people wanting you to look at their art. The only real difference between the two cities is that New York is great for creating art and Los Angeles is great at selling it. By transitive properties if you can make LA work for you then you've somehow succeeded artistically. At least that's how I see it.

While living in Los Angeles I tried my hand at a lot of things including but not limited to the topics in the next few chapters. Some failures were more spectacular than others. Some hurt more than others. Los Angeles wasn't as cruel to me as it has been to others but it was still pretty mean.

Chapter 4: Failing at Writing

On the last day of my junior year of high school it hit me that I had no plans after I graduated. At the time I did the only thing I knew how to do; I wrote a poem. By then it had been about 10 years since I had attempted poetry. When I was about 6 I wrote my mom poems and left them on her bed for her to read. One day I wrote a poem that included the line "if you ever go away." My parents called me into the kitchen to question me about it. I assume that they thought I was talking about her dying or them getting divorced. I didn't mean anything by it but I could tell by their tones they thought I knew something that I shouldn't. The whole ordeal shook me up so bad that I didn't write another poem until I was 16 and in an existential crisis.

When I did start writing poems again I never showed them to anyone. They were probably terrible. How could they not be? I was a manically depressed teenager who had never actually *read* poetry. I assumed that writing poetry was just writing your emotions as they came to you and moving to the next line after the third or fourth word. That's the problem with writing. It's too easy to get started. There are no chords to learn, no special equipment to buy and no gatekeeper you have to pay off. All you need is ink and paper.

After a year of writing I saw an ad in a magazine that said if my poem was good enough I could get it bound and published in a writers anthology. All I had to do was pay for the book. Well, why didn't you say so! Of course I would pay for the book. It had my name in it. I picked my most compelling piece and sent it in.

I remember waiting with bated breath for my book to arrive and was ecstatic when it finally reached my doorstep. It was beautifully bound with gold embossed lettering. I immediately flipped to the table of contents to find my name. I remember staring at my name in disbelief for a few moments. I was finally in print! People all over the world were looking at my name in print. Maybe at the exact same time that I was.

I told everyone at my church about the big achievement. Everyone wanted me to photocopy it and sign it for them. It wasn't until then that it hit me; unless their name was in the table of contents with all the other suckers no one in their right mind would ever pay money for this book. No one was looking at my name; everyone was looking at their own. I fell for the ol' "Who's Who in America" scam. I don't even think the book had a bar code.

This didn't stop me from writing poetry though. By the time I was 19 I decided that I had enough poems to publish a collection. I didn't have a home computer so I had to go to my schools' library and copy the handwritten work onto a 3.5 high-density floppy disk.

In 2001 I self-published my first and only book of short stories and poetry entitled *The Bleeding*. When creating the cover art I asked to have a pen dripping blood onto a blank sheet of paper. The closest thing they had was a pen dripping blood onto a blank check. This would not be the last time I neglected the importance of cover art.

Another thing I neglected was my marketing budget. Even if this book were worth reading, which it wasn't, it didn't matter because no one knew that it existed and I didn't have enough money to make that happen. I thought that I could sell them to my friends and family out the trunk of my car like Too $hort. This never worked because anytime I told someone I had written a book they looked at me in astonishment and asked if they could get a free copy. To this day I've probably sold about 20 copied of *The Bleeding*.

Still, this didn't stop me from self-publishing another book in 2008. This time it was a novel called *Girl Friends*. This book I actually liked but I haven't read it in a while so it's possible that it's complete drivel. The worst part about my experience with *Girl Friends* is that I didn't fix any of the mistakes I made the first time around with *The Bleeding*. I tried a little harder to get a marketing campaign behind it but in the end I just didn't have the money. I also decided on a terrible cover and I might not have made the best decision with the title. For the cover I told the art department that I wanted a collage of women on the cover. This was because the story is about a guy that has a lot of "girl friends". Get it? From the title they took it as a story about a group of girls that bonded one summer at sleep-away camp. The cover they sent back to me was not so much a collage as four yearbook photos of beautiful women over a mauve background. I showed my coworker this and she asked me why all the women where white. I in turn asked them to add more ethnic women on the cover but that was the only change I made and if anyone had bought the book I might have regretted it. I had failed to catch fire once again but hey, at least I wrote a novel.

Well, technically *Girl Friends* was a novella. It wasn't until I was halfway finished writing this book you're reading that I did my research and learned that a book has to be 60,000 words or more. Let me rephrase that: If you are a first time author no one is going to publish your book unless you hand him or her at least 60,000 words. I always believed, like I think most people do, that you just wrote until you were finished. I didn't know that there were rules and standards. I though people became artist because they didn't want to abide by rules and standards. Go figure.

Writing a specific amount of words has always been a problem for me. In high school when I was assigned a 500 word essay I would always panic. My modus operandi in writing, as well as in life, is to tell any story I'm telling as briefly as possible.

Listen, you don't want to read the essay and I don't want to write it. We both read the chapter why do I need to go into so much detail? How about I give you a few main points to prove that I read it and we'll call it a day.

This never worked. It only made it worse when I wrote filler sentences in my papers such as "I'm only including this sentence so that I can reach the 500 word mark" and "Decisions, decisions, decisions, what do I tell you about next?" Since I self-published my first book in 2001 people have told me that they too wanted to write a book. From now on the only advice I will give them is this: if you're not prepared to write at least 60,000 words don't ever say that again.

...

I wrote my first music review in the summer of 2000 for the Christian bookstore I worked for. I don't remember the exact words but I was reviewing a Christian rock album so I'm pretty sure it was a negative review. My boss was not a fan of my review and I didn't blame him. How could he make money if I was telling everyone that his product sucked? I never wrote anything for him again but that was the first time I seriously thought about music journalism as a career.

Years later after I moved to LA I started writing articles and music reviews for various websites. My approach was pretty straightforward. I contacted people whose music I respected and asked them if I could interview them. I did phone, instant message and email interviews with artist like Nicolay, Graph Noble, Big Lez and SantiGold who was then known as Santi White the lead singer of the punk band Stiffed. I then took these interviews and sold/gave them to any website that would print them. Some websites commissioned me to interview artist, which is why I also interviewed artist like Rick Ross and Drag-on. I remember those two interviews vividly because they both went spectacularly wrong.

The Rick Ross interview was part of a press junket where we were given a number to call at a specific time where we could talk to him for exactly 10 minutes. He was never rude but it was pretty obvious that by the time I called he was tired of answering questions. He responded to each question with either a one-word answer or a canned response about hustling and making money. Keep in mind that this was 2006 and all Rick Ross had under his belt was a feature on a deep album cut by Trick Daddy.

By minute 5 I ran out of things to ask and ended the interview early. After the interview was over I took the next few hours to craft a one-page article that talked mostly about his past and what to expect from his new record *Port of Miami*. I turned it in and a few hours later I received an email asking me for a straight Q & A. I was a little hurt. I took 5 minutes of

Rick Ross' mild musings about getting money and turned it into something that human beings would actually want to read. After my many hours of hard work and research I ended up taking about 20 minutes to cobble together a coherent interview. I was expecting them to see the error in their ways and realize that the previous version was the better read. That never happened. Instead they posted it a few days later and then asked me if I wanted to conduct a phone interview Drag-on.

I agreed mostly out of curiosity. It had been 2 years since he put out any music and 6 years since anyone bought any of it. Because I was a fan I was interested in seeing what he was up to. He seemed to be in good spirits if not a little desperate. We talked about his upcoming plans and what he had been doing for the previous few years. He seemed like a really nice guy and only expressed bitterness when referring to Lil' Wayne. This was because Lil' Wayne was just starting to break into the mainstream using a moniker that Drag-on previously used: Fireman. He didn't seem to be truly mad about the "Fireman" thing; in all honestly it seemed more like sour grapes. And who could blame him? In 2000 he and Lil' Wayne were peers with gold selling albums: *The Opposite of H2O* and *Lights Out,* respectively. In a few short years Wayne was considered the greatest of his generation while Drag-on wasn't even considered. It had to be a tough adjustment and all in all he was doing pretty well. At the end of the interview he let me know that he appreciated everything and we hung up.

This is where things went slightly wrong. I'm terrible at taking notes but I didn't own a digital recorder so I recorded our conversation by holding a microphone up to the telephone and recording it on my computer. I played back what I had recorded and immediately panicked when I realized that the microphone never picked up his voice. I had to write the whole article from memory. When I turned it in I felt like I let Drag-on down. Here was his chance to tell the world that he was still alive and I screwed up the recording. But in the end no one cared. My little article on a website wasn't going to revive his career. Drag-on himself probably never ever read it. I still felt

pretty bad about it though.

I also wrote tons of music reviews. Sometimes I would

go to shows and review performances but most of the time I

reviewed albums. The upside was that I receiving more free

music that I knew that to do with. The downside is that 2000-

2010 was the worst decade in hip-hop history.

Because of this a lot of my reviews were for rock and

folk artist. My favorite review was for the album *A Sea of Tiny

Lights* from the band Nathan Lawr and the Minotaur's. I wrote

a glowing 200-word review detailing all the beautiful nooks and

crannies of the record. Unfortunately, I misread the names in

the liner notes and mentioned that Nathan Lawr made music

with his brother, which wasn't true. Nathan read the review

and berated me in the comments section for my lack of

journalist integrity. I couldn't help but feel that he was missing

the point. Furthermore if he had emailed us that we had made

a mistake it could have been easily taken care of. Why he

chose the comment section to do this was a mystery. My

guess is that he shared the mentality of most Internet commenters; something being right isn't as important as proving someone else is wrong. This general attitude is probably the biggest drawback to posting anything on the Internet and why it became so hard to want to do it anymore.

At my busiest I was writing for 6 or 7 websites. Less than half of them paid me and the ones that did were paying me less and less as the months went by. Factor in that no one was visiting these websites and this whole thing was starting to feel a lot like work. After about 2 years I decided to call it quits and guess what? No one cared.

Chapter 5: Failing at Engineering

When I first moved to California I lived in in Woodland Hills, which for the uninitiated is nowhere near Hollywood which was where the studio was. I only moved there because it was the first place I found that I could afford. I had to be at the studio at 8 AM every morning to start cleaning the bathrooms and making coffee. Because I didn't have a car I had to take the bus. It took me a few days to get it right but I eventually found a route that could get me there in 2 hours.

The studio owners were three guys that didn't seem to know or care about the music business. The idea that they could be friends with musicians seemed to be enough motivation for them. One owner would rent a Bentley whenever he knew an important client was coming. Another would namedrop like he had turrets syndrome. They were also constantly undermining each other's authority. One owner would tell me burn some demo CD's from the last session while another owner would tell me to ignore what the other owner said and order lunch for the band he booked at noon. They weren't bad guys, just middle class dudes that desperately wanted to be rich without working too hard.

Luckily I hardly saw them around much. Most of the work I did was under the tutelage of the head and assistant engineer Wade and Julio respectively. They were engineers by day and disgruntled musicians by night... and day. When no bands where booked they routinely used the studio time for their own recordings.

Downtime at the studio was the most productive for me. They would teach me about the mixing board (SSL 9000 series) and their different technics. I enjoyed being in the studio and hanging around with these guys but I knew in my heart I would never be a great engineer. The fact that I flunked out of the audio recording program would be the strongest indicator of that. But I kept my head down; kept plugging away and hopped they never noticed how awful I was at my job.

When bands came in to record I spent most of my time on the sidelines. A lot of bands already had their own engineers and when this happened Wade became the assistant engineer, Julio became the second assistant engineer and I was sent to make coffee in the lobby. This would happen on such a regular basis that I eventually became OK with it. This was also a sign that I would never be a great recording engineer.

On a typical day I would get to the studio early, make coffee, and set up the mics for the band by midday, order lunch, order dinner and then break down everything at about 1 am. And because I was over 21 I would also make the occasional alcohol run. As the days passed by I would do less setting up and more sitting in the lobby watching TV. This was when my career as a recording engineer ended.

First I'll tell you the story I tell anyone who ask why I'm no longer a recording engineer:

I was working in Hollywood and everything was going fine until one day the studio flooded. The owners didn't have flood insurance so the studio shut down and everyone lost

their jobs. I tried getting a job at another recording studio but

because of the state of the music industry in the early 2000s

and the fact that I was the lowest guy on the totem pole I

couldn't find a job and ended up working in an electronics

store.

Now I will tell you what actually happened:

One day Julio called me while I was at home and told me not to worry about coming in that day. The next day he did the same. On the third day this happed he told me not to worry about coming anymore. The worst part about it was that Wade had hired me and it should have been Wade that fired me. Instead he had Julio do it for him. I went into shock because I had never been fired before and didn't know what to do with myself. The fact that this was an internship and I wasn't being paid made me feel even worse. There was no way any recording studio would hire me so I ended up getting a job at an electronics store where I would be fired again in 3 years' time. (More on that later.)

About a year after I was fired my parents came to visit me. I was showing them the Farmers Market at The Grove in La Brea (regional!) when we ran into Wade. He told me a few months after I left that the studio flooded and everyone lost his job. I told him that I wasn't an engineer anymore and he didn't seem surprised. I appreciated that he was cool enough to mention that I "left the studio" in front of my parents. I was a recording engineer for 5 months, from October 2002 to March 2003.

I only miss being an engineer in theory. It's a cool story to tell and it's a much better job title than anything I've been called since. But the truth is I was never going to be any good at it. I had no real desire to get any better. I was just a guy hanging around a studio waiting for someone to tell me what to do. Even though it didn't last long it was fun while it did. Engineering was the thing that got me out of East Texas and for that I am eternally grateful.

Chapter 6: Failing at Rapping

After I got fired from my engineering internship I set up a home recording studio in my living room and recorded a demo. Rapping was something I had thought about doing a few years earlier but I never pursued. I was a 20+ year-old Black kid living in Los Angeles who wanted to be a rapper. The idea of that made my skin crawl. It seemed too cliché.

With my music career I decided that I would be different by walking the line between mainstream and underground. I would create a more self-depreciating character that had to take the bus to work and didn't have a truckload of girls begging to suck his dick. I would be an everyman. I would rap about being self-conscious, working menial jobs and maybe even about dropping out of college. In 2004 Kanye West beat me to the punch by releasing The College Dropout. I knew that anything I did would sound like an echo but I didn't stop recording.

I hand pressed and labeled CD-Rs and sent them to dozens of record labels. The only label that responded was Flyte Tyme Records, a label owned by Jimmy Jam and Terry Lewis. They only wrote me to let me know that they didn't record hip-hop music. Although I doubt it was actually Jimmy Jam or Terry Lewis that wrote me I was flattered that anyone would even take the time to respond. I would sometimes go to clubs and pass out CD-Rs to people standing in line outside. I posted my music on websites and kept a tally of how many listens I received that day. This task proved pretty simple because there were never many to count.

In the midst of all this I met a guy at my job that wanted to start his own cable access TV show. His show would celebrate underground hip-hop and he asked me if I would record a theme song. I jumped at the chance. I don't think he actually liked the song I gave him but I also don't think he had any other prospects. A couple of weeks later he wanted to shoot a video for the opening credits.

It was low budget affair but I was impressed by how well he pulled everything together. He hired a camera crew, dancers, make-up artist, motorcyclist, and scouted the location all by himself. Although he put a lot of work into all of this it was also obvious that he really didn't care about the music being presented on his show. He was just another hustler looking for whatever would bring money in. Although the whole affair was a little cringe worthy, I was OK with shooting a video with semi-pretty girls on motorcycles with guys posturing and flashing money. I was just glad someone noticed me.

Eventually he figured out that endorsing me wasn't going to bring him any real money and he stopped calling me to record songs with the other artist he worked with. I still have the video we recorded and even though I disagreed with sentiment, I appreciated the chance.

Using a camcorder that a friend gave me for my birthday I started recording my own music videos. The first one was for a song I titled "Popular Science". It was a song about figuring out how to become more widely accepted or more directly "the science of being popular". I shot the whole thing in my room and used the Bob Dylan trick of holding up cue cards during the song. A journalist friend of mine liked it and posted it on a website without me knowing. It received hundreds of views in a matter of days. Unfortunately the comments they left were mostly negative. It seemed my friend posted it onto a site that wasn't necessarily a music site and certainly not a hip-hop site. The Internet nerds tore it to pieces.

My biggest offense was mentioning in the video description that this song was available on my album entitled *How to Disappear Completely*. That's right, I named my rap album after a Radiohead song. One commenter pointed out my egregious act by posting a link for the "real" video for "How to Disappear Completely." Those of you that are Radiohead fans know that there is no official video for that song so that comment has always puzzled me.

A fledgling film director named David directed the Radiohead video independently. This is how I met the director for my song and video "Simple X". I figured if everyone hated my video then maybe I should get a "real" director. Because I didn't trust myself I left all the decisions up to him. The only note I gave was that I didn't want to play the lead. I barely wanted to be in the video.

The song was about a guy that spent all his time working to provide for himself only to realize that his life was passing him by. The lead character (not me) walks through life with his briefcase oblivious to all the beauty that life has to offer until he walks by a street performer (me) and has a life-affirming heart attack. You know, typical hip hop video shit.

David also wrote a scene where everything would move in reverse and in turn I would be rapping backwards a la The Pharcyde in the Spike Jonze directed "Drop" video. I practiced for hours. I played my lyrics backwards, wrote them down on notecards and practiced in the mirror. At the video shoot David had cue cards created for me. He had comedian Bret Weinbach play the lead although at the time I had no idea who he was. The rest of the cast and crew were nice and I couldn't get over the fact that everyone was there on account of me.

About a month later I received the finished product. The storyline didn't come together quite like I would have liked and apparently my backwards lyrics didn't work because they were barely used but other than that it turned out pretty well. Once I made it available for everyone to see the response was mostly positive. To this day this still my most watched video with a whopping 7,000 views but it's probably not because of the song. After a few weeks I used an analytics tool to see how long people were watching the video and at what time did they turned it off. For the first minute and a half people seemed to be engaged but shortly after everyone seemed to be losing interest. I found out that this was because for the first minute and a half Brent is the star of the show. Even when I'm rapping as long as Brent's face is shown everyone is tuned in. The 1:31 mark is the first time people see my face and in those seconds they immediately voted "no". Still, it's my most viewed video and I can't afford to look it in the mouth.

Although it was a fairly pleasant experience I decided to shoot all my other videos myself. Spending money on a video didn't sell me any records or gain me any fans. The other videos I directed for myself didn't sell me any records or gain me any fans but at least they didn't cost me any money.

Getting people to notice me was something I could never figure out. How a non-celebrity can upload something and get even one thousand people to watch it was and is unfathomable to me. Successful people will tell you that the secret is to work hard and eventually your hard work will pay off. The problem with this statement is that we're only asking "successful people". In research this is called Selection Bias. This statement doesn't take into account all the hard workers struggling in obscurity.

Everyone loves to hear about a person's dedication and hard work but luck doesn't get the credit it deserves. That's because luck is like a force of nature. You can thank your parents. You can thank your coworkers. You can even thank yourself. You can't thank a force of nature. You can't thank the wind. You can thank the Gods of wind (the Anemoi) but directly thanking the wind is crazy talk. No Oscar winner has ever gone up to the podium and thanked Luck for helping them write the movie based on their erotic fan fiction of the late nineties workplace sitcom NewsRadio. At least not until I finish writing the screenplay.

I, on the other hand, think luck is just as important as anything else. Luck is the hardest thing to accept because it's the only part of the equation that you can't control. You can be born with a certain amount of talent and improve but you can't change your luck. You can replace the word luck with God but that may make matters even worse: the last person to change God's plan was Noah and the rest of the planet suffered pretty righteously for that one.

After about 4 years of having a cursory rap career I decided to be more proactive and set some goals. I gave myself a year. I wasn't looking to become a megastar. I just wanted to book some shows, sell some CD's, or get some real views to my videos and website. I decided to put everything I had into one year and if I could get even a few of those goals accomplished I would continue. If I was still in the same place a year later I knew it would be time for me to quit.

I auditioned for shows, I sold CD's on the bus, held contest, gave away T-shirts on my website and contacted record labels every evening. After 6 months I was completely burnt out. I couldn't take being that extroverted. I decided to split the difference and only be a self-aggrandizing lunatic half the time. At the end of the year nothing had changed. No one visited my website, no one watched my videos, and no one booked me for a show. Maybe I wasn't talented. Maybe I didn't work hard enough. Maybe I wasn't lucky. The only thing I knew was that I liked making music and that I was going to keep making music until it wasn't fun anymore. And that's exactly what I did.

I once recorded a theme song for a podcast called Get Up Off This with Matt Robinson (the podcast within the podcast Get Up On This with Jensen Karp). They were accepting submission every week and played anything they got. When they finally played mine I was ecstatic. They gave out my Twitter handle and I waited patiently for the world to

realize my genius. No one ever did and that was the last song

I ever recorded.

Chapter 7: Failing at Comedy

My dad used to love Hip-Hop. Let me rephrase that: my dad didn't always deride hip-hop as the music of the Devil. In the late 80s when Hip-Hop was becoming more of a staple of contemporary music my dad was 30; too old to truly understand it but still young enough to appreciate it. I remember one rainy night my dad taking me to a record store to buy the Krush Groove soundtrack. To this day I couldn't tell you if he was buying it for himself or me. He appreciated the LL Cool J's, the Run DMC's, and even though the Beastie Boys may have been a little too punk rock for him he got the sentiment. But the late 80s brought West Coast Gangsta Rap and by then all bets were off. The older and more religious he got the more he hated cursing or to be more specific "music related cursing". For example he never cared for Ice Cube but loved the movie Friday. I wouldn't be surprised if he's seen the NWA biopic *Strait Out of Compton* a few times but I guarantee he's never heard the album.

My dad has always loved music though. It's one of the things I certainly got from him. A conservative estimate of his collection in it's prime would be somewhere around 300 records. He also had a 10-inch reel to reel in the living room, which was something I thought every household had. Of all the records my dad owned only 4 of them were comedy albums: Richard Pryor, Redd Foxx, Eddie Murphy and Cheech and Chong. No Bill Cosby, no Bob Newhart, no Flip Wilson. My dad's aversion to profanity always puzzled me because his comedy records were about as filthy as it gets. His entire comedy collection consisted of three of the most foulmouthed motherfuckers on the planet and two weed aficionados.

My comedy education began at the tender age of 7 with Redd Foxx's "You Gotta Wash Your Ass". I was never the same. From there my siblings flung Richard Pryor and Eddie Murphy jokes to each other like they were Shakespearean sonnets. George Carlin was the first stand-up comedian that I discovered on my own. I was too young for the "Saturday Night Live" or the "Hippy dippy weatherman" George Carlin. I discovered him after he had gotten much darker, when he was verbally attacking children and ranting about the continuing "pussificaiton" of the American male. It was through George that I discovered that stand-up comedy actual involved work. Eddie Murphy made it seems as though he woke up every morning, slipped into a leather suit, walked up to a microphone and just started riffing about talking cars. Eddie was a party on a fancy yacht. Carlin was a swim in the East River. If you've ever met someone that has memorized an Eddie Murphy joke you could categorize him or her as a person that enjoys comedy. If you've ever met someone that has memorized a George Carlin joke that person probably suffers from Asperger's Syndrome.

When my family finally got cable I spent a lot of time with Comedy Central. In between viewings of Benny Hill, Mr. Bean and Monty Python I watched every stand up special that aired. Even though I spent hours absorbing this stuff I didn't really get it. It was mostly white men in their 30s and 40s talking about losing their hair, gaining weight, or disappointing their wife. Having said that; I must have watched Dana Carvey's "Critic's Choice" a dozen times. I also watched In Living Color, Uptown Comedy Club and Comic View religiously. We didn't have HBO so I never got to see the really big standup specials or Def Comedy Jam but even if I could watch them they cursed way too much for me to watch them in front of my parents. I could listen to a Richard Pryor record while my parents were away but most of the good stuff on HBO cam on after they got home from work.

Even though I was awash with comedy from all different angles most of the space in my brain was being taken up by music. This may be because it was easier to talk to my friends at school about Easy-E than it was to talk about David Brenner. All of this changed when I first saw The State on MTV in 1993. I watched Python and Kids in the Hall but I didn't really appreciate them. They were a little too goofy and nonsensical. The State was all those things too but they felt a little more menacing. Maybe it was the theme music or maybe it was because they always seemed to look like they had just woken up from a three-day coke binge. Whatever it was I

worshipped them like the rock stars they where. I memorized

their names, studies their various personalities and followed

their careers. It was the first time I felt like I was having a

dialog with comedy instead of just absorbing it. I felt this

feeling again a few years later when Mr. Show with Bob and

David debuted. I didn't know it at the time because the term

hadn't been created yet but I was a comedy nerd.

For whatever reason, I never put my comedy nerdom

to use. It was probably because I didn't know it could be

useful. Although I had watched hours of standup comedy as a

teen it never occurred to me that standup was something that

could be aspired to. Most middle to lower class kids only

aspired to be athletes, musicians, or actors. Not too many

people aspired to be a clown. Outside of the top three choices

the only other thing I aspired to be was a writer. Not because I

was good at writing or because I even liked writing. I just felt

that it was the best possible way to express myself. You could

write your feelings down on a piece of paper, hand it to

someone and walk out of the room. While you're writing you don't have to worry about anyone else's reaction. And you can take your time saying exactly what you wanted to say.

If I could do it all over again I most certainly would have been a comedy writer. Most of my favorite TV shows had to do with the writers room: *The Dick Van Dyke Show, The Larry Sanders Show, 30 Rock,* the first third of *Studio 60 on Sunset Strip.* In school I was never the class clown but always the sidekick; the smart kid that would tell the charismatic class clown what to say. There was one kid named Courtney that always gave me credit for my jokes and I hated it. I wanted to get my thoughts out but I couldn't stand the attention. Also, no one ever believed him when he told them that what they just laughed at was a joke I thought up. I would love to have the careers of people like Larry David, Phil Rosenthal, Neal Brennan, Jeannie Gaffigan or Ali Leroy. I revel in the thought of being second banana. (No offence to any of the people I just named. The faint praise I just heaped on you was not meant to be ironic. In all seriousness I would love to be the invisible partner in a two-person act.)

I never really thought about doing stand up comedy until I was 29 years old. I'm not sure why it took so long to hit me but I feel like it was something that's been a part of me since I was a kid. I never sought attention but whenever it was given to me I took the chance to be funny. Whether it was reading the announcements at church or presenting my book report to the class, I always felt humor should be at least a small part of any presentation. In college I used to give presentations to other students about suicide prevention. I wrote a joke about Eyore from Winnie the Pooh that killed every time.

The first time it crossed my mind that I wanted to try stand up comedy was on a night when I couldn't sleep. I looked at the ceiling and thought about what joke I would tell if I were a stand up. In 28 years of life I had never had that thought before. The first time I actually did stand up was a year later when I was in grad school. There was a talent show and I told them I was a pro. I had never done it but I was pretty sure I could. The month leading up to the show I still didn't perform. I wrote jokes and practiced in my room but I never got up on stage until my actual performance. When I finally got to the stage my first joke didn't connect but I kept going and I did pretty well but I got off stage felling pretty depressed. *Sure, they laughed but why didn't I kill?* This feeling is one I would later come to know as "being a comedian".

The first actual show I did was at a dive bar in Van Nuys, CA called Liquid Zoo. It was a variety show and I was the only comedian. When I went up the place was pretty loud. As soon as I started talking the place quieted down and it totally freaked me out. Luckily they only remained silent for about 5 seconds before everyone went back to talking, playing pool and chatting up prostitutes. I think they realized that I wasn't going to do any "black/white" humor. One guy during my set yelled out "bust a freestyle!" I didn't have the chops to come up with a witty retort. The best I could do was "Why, because I'm Black?" I got off stage that night realizing that I really hated bar shows. But of course this was far from my last bar show.

Honestly, hecklers at bars have never scared me that me that much. My true fear has always been reserved for Black women. This is not because Black women are inherently terrifying but because in adolescence everyone is terrified of the opposite sex. It just so happens that during my adolescence I was surrounded by Black girls.

I wasn't nervous around any other girls because I really didn't care what they thought of me. I wanted to be what Black girls thought was cool and I wanted to be tough like Black girls wanted me to be. I was none of those things and they let me know it as often as possible. As I got older and became more comfortable the terror subsided but it never went away.

It reared its head when I competed in a talent show at my university. (Not the same talent show at my university where I did my first set. This was months later.) The crowd was about 70 freshmen. About 40 of them were Black women. At least 20 of those Black women were in the front row. I got to the show early and when I saw them walk in one after the other I panicked. It was like being in junior high all over again. Thankfully by the time I got to the mic I was completely calm. Unfortunately that calmness didn't help me connect with any of them. They answered all my rhetorical questions, shouted out their own punch lines, and at one point requested I do a Steve Harvey impression. After enduring this for about 5 minutes it occurred to me that I wasn't' going to win the talent show so I started in with my atheist material. A few girls walked out but not before I could tell them "God bless you" which got a laugh for some reason.

As far as the other contestants were concerned there wasn't much competition. Third place was a guy who wrote a poem for his girlfriend and second place was a comedian who wasn't funny but apparently invited all his friends to see him. The guy who got first place did it by spouting pop culture references and starting every joke with "remember when". This clearly wasn't my crowd but I was OK with that. When I was on that stage and behind the mic I wasn't terrified anymore. It was like the mic was a bulletproof shield. I knew I belonged up there and I didn't have any regrets except for not having a decent Steve Harvey impression up my sleeve.

...

If you only learn one thing from going to an open mic it should be that no one knows what he or she are doing. No matter what conversation you overhear, or how confident a person looks, or how many friends this person seems to have, everyone there is at the same level of incompetence. If they knew what they were doing they wouldn't be waiting in line at an open mic. Unless you see someone walk up to the host and say, "Can I do some time?" then that person is an armature just like you.

Comedians that didn't take open mics seriously always bothered me. Most open mics are done by lottery so I always considered myself lucky to be on stage time I always came with material I wanted to test out. I always hated it when the comedian clearly didn't care that they were on stage and just rambled though their sets. I always treated the open mic like a gym. Comics that don't have anything prepared are like the person that goes to the gym, does 10 curls, looks at their phone for 5 minutes and then does 10 more curls. As far as I was concerned every second of stage time you get is to be cherished.

In case you didn't know open mics are almost always full of comedians. You're lucky if you ever get a "real" person in the audience. The worse part of open mics is sitting through 60-90 minutes of mediocre comedy. As painful as it was at times I always tried to actually listen to the other comedians and not just focus on what I was going to say when I had my chance. I always loved it when I heard someone with a great joke or a unique way of presenting an old topic. Some nights my only joy was going up to people after the show to tell people which of their jokes I liked. I don't know if this is just an LA thing or not by my enthusiasm never seemed to be shared by anyone else. When I did shows I had crown members tell me they liked my jokes but never at open mics.

...

One night I went to a show at the Hollywood Improv. It was the first time I had been in that room and had a good time. That's because I wasn't performing. I came to the show because one night I was watching Louie CK's TV show Louie and saw a comedian I didn't recognize. I was thrown off because the guy doing stand up was clearly a pro but I had never seen him before. My Comedy Nerd ego was feeling bruised so I looked him up and found out his name was Alan Havey and that he was doing a show in LA the following week. The show had a great line up: Greg Fitzsimons, Andy Kindler, Sarah Silverman, Dom Irrera, Jerrod Carmichael, and hosted by Allen Havey. This is a lineup that could only happen in LA or New York.

Jerrod Carmichael was the only performer I didn't know beforehand. This was maybe a year before the world realized how great he was and gave him his own TV show. After the show was over I went to the men's room, as I'm at the urinal this guy reaches for the door to leave, and as he opens the door he looks over to me and says "Great show." Shortly after the words leave his lips he says, "Oh, you're not the guy." It took me a moment to realize what had just happened; he thought I was Jerrod Carmichael. Honest mistake, we *were* the only two Black guys in the room. The way he said it I honestly couldn't tell if he was joking or not. After thinking about it for a few hours, I realized he probably wasn't but I was flattered nonetheless. That's the first complement I had ever received in that building. The only thing that brought down my mood was when a lady waiting for her car from the valet didn't know who Dom Irrera was and was surprised when she found out he was funny. How do you not know Dom Irrera?

...

After a few years my comedy boner began to sag. I still loved stand up. In fact the 5-15 minutes I spent on stage were some of the greatest moments in my life. Everything outside those 5-15 minutes killed any desire I had to become any better. My age played a big roll. It's really hard to hang out with 20 year olds when you're not 20. Let alone 20-year-old Los Angelinos that want to be professional comedians.

The following equation describes what it's like to be a "young" comedian in Los Angels:

[(The wisdom that comes with getting older - The life experience to support said wisdom) +need for constant affirmation] * 50 = Inside of any comedy club on open mic night

Much like drug addiction, comedy can be very taxing. Having to go out every night of the week to sit in a club or a bar for 3 or more hours in the hopes that I could get on stage for 5 minutes was starting to take its toll. In cities like New York you can go from bar to bar doing sets. In Los Angeles after you're done at one place you have to drive across town to get to the next place. You could be out all night and only do 10 minutes. The other option was to make nice with some up and coming comedians that where creating there own shows in bars and basements around town but I've already told you how I feel about 20-year-olds.

Also much like drug addiction, comedy requires 100% of your time. I was in grad school. You can trip, fall and land into an Associated Degree. You can half ass a Bachelor Degree. But anything beyond that, you're either in or you're out and in LA comedy is nearly impossible to do as a hobby. By the age of 30 I had already restarted my life twice. Was I really ready to do it a third time?

So I made the decision to stop doing stand up. Sure, I could have chosen to do comedy on the side but doing that wouldn't have made me a better comedian. I would have been stuck doing open mics and free bar shows. I never would have reached the next level. So I'll never become a 'comedian' because I respect the profession far too much to call myself that. I'll always just be a guy that did comedy for a few years.

To be honest I never had particularly high hopes for my comedy career. I would be happy if I could just have the career of Jerry Seinfeld. Not Jerry Seinfeld the co-creator of Seinfeld mind you but "Jerry Seinfeld" the TV character. He could afford a big apartment on the Upper West Side, buy a new couch when he wanted, had enough food to feed him and his next-door neighbor, had enough money to buy his parents a Cadillac, to own a Black Saab convertible, to pay $50 for a marble rye, to date a different beautiful woman every week, and he didn't have a day job. He did it all just by telling jokes. TV Jerry Seinfeld was living every comedian's dream. Also, he never locked his apartment door, which is the kind of America I'd like to live in.

Chapter 8: Failing at Los Angeles

When I was about 10 I went to a high school football game with one of my brothers, my sister and my aunt. I wasn't particularly interested in the game so I wondered into the woods behind the bleachers. I picked up a soda can that had been cut open and accidently sliced my finger. I was cut pretty bad but it didn't seem life threatening. I stood there watching the blood drip from my finger onto a tree stump for about 3 minutes. Eventually my brother walked by and asked me what was going on. He came over and helped me clean and bandage it. I doubt my brother remembers this story but I do because there's one thing about it that I still find odd. It's not that I stood there for 5 minutes with a bloody stump, it's that the idea of stopping the bleeding or asking for help never occurred to me.

...

I originally came to California because I got an internship as a recording engineer and after 6 months my dream fizzled. I immediately applied for any jobs available and set out to becoming a responsible adult. Moving back to Texas was never an option. When I say that I don't mean that it was an option and then I took it off the table. I mean it literally never occurred to me that I could pack up and move back to Texas. Like so many times before, I took what was given to me and tried to make the best of it.

When I arrived in Los Angels I had roughly $200 to my name after I paid my 3 new roommates $400 for rent. I was still waiting on my last paycheck from my job in Orlando plus I had my deposit from my rental truck to look forward to so I was pretty set. I had roughly 3 weeks before I had to scrape up another $400 so things were looking up.

I had my paycheck forwarded to my parent house since I didn't know where I would be living when I moved. When my parents received my check they cashed it and mailed me a personal check. At least that was the story they told me. It really didn't matter because the check never got to me because my parents got my address wrong. I now had about 2 weeks to scrape up $400.

One week later my parents wired me the money with an additional $75 for my troubles. Unfortunately it wasn't enough to pay rent and utilities so I had to ask my roommate for a loan. After an incredibly uncomfortable week I was able to pay him back. After paying him back I had $7.41 to my name and about 3 weeks to scrape together $400.

My parents later sent me money so that I could open a bank account. This would have been really nice of them if their check hadn't bounced and cause me to be charged an over drafting fee which lead to my rent check bouncing which lead to another awkward discussion with my new roommates. My first few months in Los Angeles I lost about 10 lbs. due to anxiety, fatigue and not being able to afford food.

The recording studio where I worked was in Hollywood. After being fired the only time I ever spent time in this area again was when my out of town friends and family came to visit me and wanted to see the Walk of Fame. After about ten years went by I almost forgot that I used to spend 12 hours a day there every day for 3 months. Hollywood was my first impression of Los Angeles.

Years after I initially arrived, failed at Los Angeles and when back to school, I got an interview at a university in Pennsylvania. I wasn't getting many job offers so I accepted the interview. I went shopping for a suit in West Hollywood a few miles away from my old recording studio. On my way back home I decided to stop by the building to see my old stomping grounds. Once I set my foot on the curb everything came rushing back: the corner store where I used to go on beer runs for the head engineer, the donut shop where I had breakfast if I got to the studio early, the keypad that I couldn't believe they gave me the combination to. I walked up to the building and peeked at the people in the windows working away. The shingle over the door said that this building was now the Funny or Die studios. Like me, the building had also made the transition from music to comedy.

I got back in my car and as I pulled off I was overcome with a wave of sadness. I came to the entertainment capital of the world and now I was leaving empty-handed. I felt like I had squandered this enormous gift. If I had tried a little harder I could have been one of the people that helped this city get it reputation. My name could have been in the credits. Instead I was moving to Pennsylvania to pursue my plan B. I thought I had accepted the fact that I was not going to be in the entertainment industry. Seeing the studio again made me realize that I hadn't. Moving away would put the final nail in the coffin. I would never attain my dream.

I never got the job in Pennsylvania and I still haven't moved away. I probably will one day. I'm actually looking forward to it. After I've had a few years to think about it I've come to accept the fact that I'll always be a creative person. I just might never get paid for it.

Part III: Failing at Everything Else

I wish I could say that I only failed at school and art and that everything else was smooth sailing. Actually I don't. If that were true I would only have half a book. The truth is I'm just getting started. So, here we go!

Chapter 9: Failing at Women

The following is a detailing of my interactions with various women in my life. I would like to tell you that the names have been changed to protect the innocent but truth be told some of their names I can't remember. I would also like for you to note that this is not a complete list and that I had sex with none of these women. A complete list of women that have rejected me deserves it's own book and the list of women I actually did sleep with could hardly be considered a list at all.

...

The Girl Next Door

My first kiss was when I was about 5. It was with the girl that lived across the fence from me. Our back yards touched. Sorry, that kind of sounded like innuendo. What I mean to say is that we were neighbors. She talked a lot about her dad and knew more about the male body than I did. When I think about it now she was probably being sexually abused. I think about her from time to time and hope that wasn't the case.

...

The Fat Girl

I didn't get much action again until I was in college but I gave it a try as early as junior high. It seemed like none of the girls I liked would even talk to me. I can only recall one girl that I liked that also seemed to like me back. Her name was Tracey. When my friends found out one of them asked "Tracey? The fat girl?" I was stunned because she wasn't skinny but I would never go so far as to call her fat. I don't even remember the guys' name that said it but because of his comments I never talked to her again. By the next year she was dating someone else and I was hurt because that guy cold have been me. From then on I decided I was going to be more open-minded when it came to women or at lease less easily swayed by popular opinion.

...

My First Girlfriend

I didn't have my first girlfriend until I was 18. The kicker is that I graduated high school when I was 17. I was a freshman in college the first time I *really* kissed a girl. I was raised to be respectful of women and with my first girlfriend I may have been too respectful. She always asked me over to her apartment when her dad wasn't home. One time she even took a shower while I was there. While I was sitting in her living room respecting her privacy I'm pretty sure she wanted me to join her. I knew this because afterwards she asked me why I didn't join her. As the months passed she grew tired of my respectfulness and I grew tired of wondering if I should make a move. She went away for a week to visit family and while she was gone I never though about her once. When she got back she clearly wasn't interested anymore and the feeling was mutual. I don't think we ever officially broke up. We just stopped seeing each other.

…

The Older Woman

The next summer while working as a telemarketer (apologies all around) I had a flirty work relationship with the older women that sat next to me. She was probably only about

25 but when you're 19 any female over 21 is Mrs. Robinson. The great thing about it was that she flirted back. She went so far as to suggest we go out to her car and have a go. To this day I have never been so obsessed with having sex with another living person. I'm convinced that my life would have been totally different had she taken me seriously. She never did and when I lost my virginity a few months later I thought of her.

...

The Ugly Girl

After Tracey from junior high I was always proud of myself for being attracted to women of different shapes and sizes. I felt I was more evolved because I didn't have "type". The truth is I didn't have enough confidence to have a "type". I was just happy to be with whomever wanted me but my diffidence did have its limits.

Brittney was a girl I met my first year away at college who was smart, funny, and a proud nerd. None of these things attracted me to her though. What attracted me the most was the fact that she was enamored with me. At the same time my ego would never let me get past the fact that Britney bore a striking resemblance to Leon Spinks.

Her courting of me started on a field trip my Communications class took to the local TV station. We were in a van and she sat a few rows behind me. With no prompting she asked me from the back of the van if my girlfriend was also a Communications major. I looked back a little freaked out but answered that I didn't have a girlfriend. She claimed she couldn't hear me and asked if she could come up and sit beside me. Before I knew it she was reading my palm and had her head on my shoulder. I, along with everyone else in the van, was a little weirded out but none of us intervened. My loneliness wouldn't allow me to turn down a strangers company.

When we got back to campus she asked me for a ride home. We went back to her place and talked for a few hours. After she lit a candle, took off her glasses and sat next to me on the bed my shallowness trumped my solitude and I decided it was time for me to go home. The next day our mutual friend Gladys who was also in the van with us asked what happened the night before. I told her that nothing happened; we talked and I went home. I left out the part about her sitting uncomfortable close to me. Gladys then informed me that Britney regaled her of the enchanting evening she and I spent together. I decided then that this had to be put to an end. Fortunately Britney had enough self-esteem for the both of us and before I mentioned anything she backed down and moved on to her next conquest.

...

My First Love

Nicole was the first girl I ever fell in love with. She lived down the hall from me while I was away at college. She was tall, thin and was what Black people like to call "Red-Boned". She basically looked like Anne-Marie Johnson. I was originally a friend of her roommate but when I came over every evening everyone knew I was headed to Nicole's room. When I was having a good day I would come over and she would celebrate with me. When I was having a bad day I would come over and she would console me. As my college career dragged on my bad days increased and before long all I did was go to her room to grouse about my increasing bad luck. I was convinced that I was in love with her and every day I went to her room, sat on her bed and broke my own heart.

At first I tried to hide my feelings but after a few months I finally told her how I felt. She told me she didn't feel the same but that we could still be friends. I was satisfied with being her friend for a while until I wasn't and then I told her I loved her again a few months later. Of course she turned me down again. My non-relationship with Nicole also coincided with one of the darkest periods in my life. In my eyes she was the only good thing about waking up in the morning. There were days where the only time I left my room was to see her. I knew when she got out of class and I would walk down the hall to greet her practically every day. I realize now that she probably hated me but back then when I looked in her eyes all I saw was the girl that was going to save my life.

Speaking of saviors she was also a devout Christian. In fact the first time we met was when we both joined the same church on the same day. After I joined I never went again but she went every Sunday. She tried to convince me of gods' divine plan but I was never persuaded. I was content to wallow in my misery. This is not to say that I was just kvetching. I was going through a deep depression, I was flunking out of school, I was being kicked out of my apartment, and I thought that if she would just love me it would all go away. She was the only person in my life that could console me and her reward for being a good listener was my being infatuated with her. In my mind this was what love was. I believe in psychology this is what they call transference.

When I decided to move to Florida she was the only person I told. I'm sure she was relieved to get rid of me though I couldn't tell at the time. After I got to Florida she was the first person I called. Around the time I moved to Florida was also the time my first book was published. In it I wrote a short story about our non-relationship entitled *Like Friends Do*. It started on page 14 and ended on page 17. It started "Like a child he waved at her as she walked away" and got worse from there. It was about the night I first told her I loved her. It ended with a quote from the Oakland rap duo The Coup. It was awful.

Nevertheless I wrote a letter to her telling her to read it. After I mailed the letter I didn't hear from her for about a month. After a month of waiting by the telephone I finally called her and she told me that she wrote me a letter back but apparently I never got it. I have no idea if she ever actually bought the book and read the story but it didn't matter because she said her feelings hadn't changed about me and she let me know that we couldn't be friends any longer. She could no longer be a friend to someone who wasn't "saved".

For exactly one week Nicole and I weren't friends and I was miserable. I threw away everything I had that reminded me of her except for the picture of her I kept in my wallet. It was years before I got rid of that picture. After our last phone call I wrote Nicole a letter telling her how hurt I was with her decision. She called me after she got it. When she called I had a friend over so I didn't pick up the phone but when I saw her name on my Caller ID I froze. She left a message that said she wanted to apologize. After my friend left I called her back and she said she was sorry that she hurt me and that maybe we could be friends. A week and one day after that call she called me again to tell me that she had reconsidered her decision. We could no longer be friends. No take backs.

It wasn't until then that I realized how draining our relationship had been on her. She was just trying to be a good person and I was taking advantage of her. I cried myself to sleep, I woke up the next morning feeling like I had an appendage removed but after the day was over I moved on. The last few months of my life had been so rocky that this felt like just another unfortunate thing that had happened to me. To this day I still get warm feelings when I think about her. I pored out my heart to her for 3 straight semesters and she never complained. That has to be worth something.

...

My Work Wife

Jessica and I worked together at Wal-Mart and everyone who knew us assumed we were dating. If anyone ever asked her she would say that we were just friends. If anyone ever asked me I would tell them to ask her because all the evidence I saw pointed to her being interested in me.

At the time I was living with my cousin and we were sharing a phone line because that's what people did back then. Dozens of times my cousin would be on the phone and Jessica would call and ask for me. My cousin would always tell her to call back in 30 minutes and like clockwork she would call back in 30 minutes. My cousin of course would still be on the phone and would tell her to call back in another 30 minutes and that is exactly what she did. This would have made sense if she had something terribly important to tell me but she never did. She just wanted to talk.

At work she would schedule our breaks and lunches together and would come and find me if I appeared to be missing. She made sure our work schedules were always the same but this could have been because she needed a ride.

Apparently she enjoyed spending every possible minute with me unless those minutes were spent being more than friendly. She even agreed to meet my family when I went home for Thanksgiving but backed out the day before.

Every now and then she would bring up a guy that she had a crush on to hint that she wasn't interested but I didn't buy it. The truth was that I wasn't that head over heels for her either but I figured as long as we were in proximity we might as well give it a try. But I never got a chance to wear her down because over the winter break she had to go back home to Jamaica and I never saw her again. She somehow got my number after I moved to Orlando and we talked a few times but we eventually lost touch. Maybe a long distance relationship was too much for her.

...

The Married (Almost) Woman

A few years later after I moved to Orlando, FL I met Yazmin. At my school, boys outnumbered girls 10 to 1 so the first thing that attracted me to her was that she was in fact a she. She got bonus points because she was also Black. In a sea of White faces this had to be destiny.

I'm not sure how we first began talking but it didn't take long for us to become friends. We remained no more than friends because Yazmin also had a fiancé. She assured me that they would be moving in together in a few months. Maybe it was just my jealousy but around me she never seemed to behave like a person that was about to get married to the love of her life.

Case in point she told me that her fiancé had to sit on the porch for a month before he could come inside her home. I was in her apartment about 3 days after I met her and we stayed up until 3am talking. She actually didn't call her fiancé that night because she was talking to me, which I have to admit I'm a little proud about. That night she also told me that I looked like Usher. Moments later she told me that she had a crush on Usher. So by transitive property that means she has a crush on me, right? Right? Also her fiancé was only 18. She was 20. Who falls in love with an 18-year-old boy?

One day I came how to find that she left 2 long ambiguous messages on my answering machine. I called her back to find out what she was talking about and it turned out she couldn't be friends with me anymore because she didn't believe that she was behaving like a woman that was about to marry the love of her life. Five days later she called me to ask if she could stay with me for a few days because she was being kicked out of her apartment. She told me that after a few days she would move back up north with her fiancé and then after a month they would both move back to Orlando but right now she had no place to stay.

Somehow I was the only person she knew and trusted so she asked me and I had no good reason to turn her down. I gave her my futon while I slept on the couch but in the middle of the night I snuck into bed with her. She woke up a little surprised but didn't object. I never touched her and I remained on top of the covers the whole time. I spent the next hour deciding what I should do next and fell asleep before I could come up with anything.

I woke up the next morning to her on top of me. Not in a sexual way. It was more like when Nala pinned Simba in The Lion King. It was playful. At lease I'm assuming that's how she meant because she immediately rolled off me once she woke me up.

Later on while she was using the bathroom mirror I moved in beside her and tried to kiss her. I put my hand on the side of her face and moved in close. In the movies this would have been the moment that we locked eyes and kissed but she pulled away. I felt ashamed and I feel even more ashamed now because I don't remember if I ever apologized. We silently agreed to pretend that it never happened and went about our day.

Her boyfriend moved to Orlando shortly after this and we never spoke again. The fact that he never hunted me down was probably proof that she never told him that she spent the night at my place or that I tried to kiss her. She was also a devout Christian so I probably dodged a bullet.

...

My Lolita

I went to my first concert when I was 22. It was Nas. The opener was Ali from the St. Lunatics. It was also the first time I danced with a girl at a club. Technically it was the House of Blues in Walt Disney World Resort in Orlando Florida but you get the idea.

I danced with her all night. The whole time she was rubbing her ass against my zipper all I could think was how beautiful her back was. When her purse fell off her shoulder I picked it up. When she looked dehydrated I offered to buy her water. She declined which was good for me because water was $2.50 a bottle.

In my mind I was finally becoming a stud. This girl and me were going to exchange numbers and talk on the phone and go out to dinner. She might even come back to my place tonight. Her girlfriends put an end to that immediately.

At the end of the night she wanted to go backstage. When we got to the entrance the security guard, recognizing that she was a pretty girl in a tight dress, let her through with no hesitation. I was stopped for some reason. She told me to wait for her and that she'd be right back. Her girlfriends also stayed behind. After she left they informed me that she had a boyfriend and I felt a little confused. Why was she wasting her time dancing with me and why wasn't he there? They told me that he was. My mojo was completely drained. I thought I finally figured out how play the game and it turned out that I was the same loser I had always been. But here's the kicker: they also informed me that she was 15. I felt physically ill. I did an about-face and headed to the nearest bus stop to catch a ride home so I could scrub myself clean and tried to forget that this night ever happened.

...

The Long Distance Relationship

My Engineering degree was a 12-month program. I met Lena when I was in my 11th month of school. She was in her second. What made this situation different from most others was that she was actually interested in me. By then it had been about 5 years since that was the case. Unfortunately we could never get any real alone time together because of our work/school schedules. I know what you're thinking, *"You're delusional. It was all in your head. Clearly she just said she was busy so that she didn't have to hang out with you."* Well on my graduation day she offered to skip class so that she could see me walk across the stage. She also offered help me move. Granted I didn't graduate and therefore there was no need in her coming. And my moving day got changed so I didn't need her to stop by that day either but she probably would have come. Maybe.

Anyway, before I left Orlando we did have one official sit down at a restaurant, come back to my place, date. The date went well and when I moved to LA I continued talking to her. It would be 9 more months before she would be finished with school and we were on separate ends of the country. For a number of reasons this was complete agony. The most obvious reason for my grief was the amount of time it would be before we could potentially see each other again but the worse part was the actual amount of time we were together. I finally meet someone that I liked and liked me back and I only got to be with her for two months. And after another two months of talking on the phone with her those feelings started turning into love. At least that's what my heart told me. My brain kept telling me that there was no way that this could have been love. I was in a big city where I didn't know anyone and she was a familiar voice. That was all there was to it. But my heart wouldn't stay silent and after a few months I told Lena I loved her. She chalked it up to infatuation. She was probably right but I still wasn't sure what to do with this infatuation. All I could do was hold my breath and hope that it eventually fizzled out.

I waited a few weeks before calling her again. She politely asked me if I was dating anyone, which is code for "you should move on because I'm not interested." We emailed back and forth for a while. I would email her a paragraph and she would email me a sentence. Sometimes her emails were just "Hi, I'll write you more when I get time." She almost never followed though. Also, Lena never called me the entire time I knew her. I always had to call her.

After she hadn't emailed me for a while I called her and she told me she lost my email address. Eventually my calls grew further apart and our emails did too. She told me that she was moving to LA after she graduated but I have no idea if she ever did. Eventually everything just fizzled out just like I planned.

...

My TV Girlfriend

I met Maria at a recording studio in LA. She wasn't an artist so I don't know how she ended up there but I was there because I with friends with a guy who was in a rap group. His uncle was a well-known Christian music producer so they got studio time whenever they wanted and he let me tag along.

They were not the strictest Christians. Once after a performance at a local church they immediately stepped outside to smoke a blunt. To their credit they did take one step off the church property out of respect they took one. I'm also pretty sure they were gang affiliated but who in LA isn't gang affiliated?

Anyway, one of the guys introduced me to Maria while I was working at the mixing board and I pretended to be engulfed in my work. Later in the day we got to talk and we hit it off. She told me about growing up in Belize and I told her about Texas. She laughed at my jokes and seemed impressed by my knowledge of studio equipment. She gave me her number and I called her the next day to make plans. Everything was going great until I mentioned that I didn't have a car. She told me she would call me back and when she didn't I waited a day and called her. Her brother picked up the phone and I left her a message. I finally got the hint when I called back again and her brother told me that I had just missed her.

This story bears mentioning only because this was the first and last time I started talking to a girl and immediately felt like she liked me. It happed just like it does on TV. And just like TV it was over in 23 minutes.

...

The Actress

After I decided to go back to school in LA I met Yuki in my American Political Institutions class. The class had theater seating for about 150 students and we both sat in the front row. A few times I talked to her before class and I found out that 1) she barely spoke English and 2) she was failing miserably. Surprisingly, neither of these things detracted from the fact that she was hot. We went out a few times but I'm not sure if she knew that they were dates. On our last date I went back to her apartment. We sat and talked at each other for a few minutes before her roommate came home and because it was a studio apartment it got a little crowded and I left.

Shortly after this Yuki stopped coming to class. About a month later while doing some "private research" I saw Yuki in a porno. I don't know if she dropped out of school to pursue her career or if she had been acting the whole time. What I do know is that I couldn't even close the deal with a struggling porn star.

...

The Coffee Date

Lisa was in my Behavioral Disorders class. She was beautiful, smart, and deaf. One day before class I passed her a note asking her out for coffee. She wrote me back that she didn't like coffee but would gladly have tea with me and gave me her number.

Hello, my name is Lee
I know passing a letter in class is very Junior High and I apologize but I don't know sign language. I was just wondering, assuming you're not seeing anyone, if you'd like to get coffee w/ me sometime

That's very sweet of you – I would love to have coffee with you (also I drink tea). :~ you can text me @

I spent the next few days trying to learn basic sign language but none of it really mattered. Every time I texted her she had an excuse why she couldn't meet with me and eventually I stopped trying. It didn't really bother me that much but after failing to launch with Lisa and Yuki I was starting to wonder if I had a thing for women I couldn't fully communicate with.

...

Tyler Durden

There has only been one time in my life that I saw a girl that made time slow down. Usually this is the type of thing that happens when you're a teenager but I was 26 when Jasmine crashed my Intro to Psychology class. Seeing her was like seeing a UFO or a ghost; no matter how hard I try to describe what happed, you'll never believe me. Because the class was full she had to stand until I offered her my seat. Time didn't resume its normal speed until she finally sat down. Afterwards I felt like my heart was going to come out of my chest. From that day forward I awaited her arrival to class and she always took the seat next to me.

One day I was outside on campus reading and she sat down beside me and started talking. To me! I couldn't comprehend what was happening. The most beautiful woman I had ever seen in real life was talking to me for no apparent reason. Something had to be wrong with her. I never saw her with her friends. There was never a crowd of guys around her. I started to wonder if she only existed in my head.

Imagine you were sitting on a park bench and Rosario Dawson sat down and started a conversation with you. Your first response may be "She is the even more beautiful up close" but after about 15 minutes:

"How can she possibly have enough time to pay attention to me?"

"Is someone going to steal my wallet while she distracts me?"

"Does she have a tumor on her Occipital lobe that makes me look like Idris Elba?"

There were even a handful of times that we walked to class together and we even ate lunch together once. I never even considered asking her out though. Best case scenario: we end up dating and I become so insecure that I end up murdering her on our honeymoon because she gave the bellboy an extra tip.

As the semesters went by I saw less and less of her but even when I did she was always alone except for the last few time I saw her. She was hanging out with a girl that was either a lesbian or a weightlifting and faux hawk enthusiast. If she was in fact a figment of my imagination this created way more questions than it did answers.

...

The Hand Off

Shelly was a girl that I worked with at a kitchen supply store. We liked the same bands, the same movies and we laughed at the same jokes. In my mind these were all things that should be the foundation of a romantic relationship. After a few months of doing what I considered to be flirting I decided that our friendship needed an upgrade. I wanted to ask her face-to-face but never got the nerve. I don't remember how I ever got her number but one day I called her after I got home from work and asked her out.

Her response, while a little heartbreaking, was incredibly nimble. After stating that she wasn't interested, she informed me that she was going to see her friend Mary perform at a bar in a few days. She invited me to come along all the while affirming that this wasn't to be misconstrued as anything other than a few friends hanging out. I hung up and debated whether or not I should go. I eventually decided that it would be more awkward for me not to go.

I showed up just as the show was starting, ordered a drink and made my way over to Shelly and her friends. The night was pretty uneventful. The music sounded a lot like to you would expect it to sound in a year where India.Arie was nominated for 7 Grammies. After the show was over Shelly introduced me to Mary and I left.

The next day Shelly informed me that Mary wanted my number. I called her that night when I got home and she invited me to go out with her friends the following night. We spent the evening driving around with her friends and party hopping. Everywhere we went people seemed to love her. I spent the whole night hoping that I lived up to whatever it was she saw in me a few nights before. Was I smiling enough? Did I contribute enough to the conversation? Was I interesting? Did I look like I was having a good time? Was I worthy of her admiration?

I wasn't. The truth was that I couldn't keep up with her. I wasn't as vibrant, energetic or spontaneous as her. She knew it. I knew it. And after a few weeks we knew that we were wasting each other's time.

...

My Fiancé

I met Kendra online. She came across some of my music on Myspace and decided to instant message me. (If you were born after 1990 you may have to look up what some of those words mean.) After a few days of talking she started sending me unsolicited tit-pics. Shortly thereafter we fell in love. We started talking in September and in November I met her and her son for the first time. We met so that we (minus her son) could fly to Dallas so she could have Thanksgiving dinner with my family. A bold move but it worked. My family loved her and we were nothing but smiles the whole trip. She even gave me a hand job on my parents' couch after everyone fell asleep.

By December all we did was fight. Or rather all I did was apologize. I asked if I could see her during Christmas and she refused. To this day I'm not sure what actually happened but as far as I could tell she just didn't love me anymore. One weekend I hopped on a bus to go see her at work. The only problem was that she was a nurse and I didn't know the name of the hospital where she worked. I ended up at the wrong one and had to call her to tell I was lost. The thinking was that if she felt she didn't want to be with me the least she could do was tell me to my face.

For the most part out talks had been cordial but after another month of begging she finally told me that she was through with me. When I pressed the issue she finally told me that she slept with someone else. She told me that this all happed after we had officially broken up and I chose to believe her. Even as she told me this I still wanted to work it out. I believed that we could get through it. She disagreed and we didn't talk about for about a year. Actually it was nine months. Exactly nine months. She failed to tell me that she was also pregnant. I was undeterred. I still believed that we could be a happy family, just the four of us.

By the time I put her out of my mind 4 years had passed. I wasted 4 years on a relationship that only lasted 4 months. I wish I could tell this story from her side but the truth is I have no idea what her side is. If you were to ask me what went wrong I would have to say that she liked me but just didn't love me. It took me 4 years to learn that you can't make someone love you. I appreciate the lesson but I wished I had learned it sooner.

...

The Walkabout

I also met Meza online but not from a dating service. We were both part of an online community. This particular online community specialized in "alternative pinup girls". If you liked tattoos, piercings and boobs then this was the place for you. It was a pretty soft-core affair. Whole Foods meets Hooters.

Meza wasn't a model, she just worked for the website. She also wrote graphic novels, sang, painted, did web design, and probably a million other things that made me marvel at her greatness. While most of the people that I talked to on the online community (models and mortals alike) lived in other cities, Meza lived in Los Angeles. The first time we met was at the LACMA where she laughed at me when I though Rene Magritte was a woman.

Afterwards we walked around for a few hours until we ended up at her apartment. Neither one of us planned this. We just didn't want to stop talking. I had just broken up with Kendra and was really lonely. She was the perfect person to talk to. She had the perfect balance of self-loathing and positivity that artist tend to have. And I was in desperate need of someone to talk to. When we got back to her place I expected it to be full of art projects and musical instruments. Instead it was crammed with old clothes and purchased artifacts and possessed just the faintest hint of cat piss. I don't remember if I ever saw a cat. She carved out a place for me to sit and we talked some more until she finally said

"So, what is it you want for little ol' me?"

"I don't know."

I knew what I wanted but I knew it was unfair of me to ask. What I wanted was for her to make me feel OK again. That's a lot to put on someone that you only met face to face a few hours ago. We ended up lying in bed together looking at the ceiling. She told me that she had a tattoo of a key on her chest. I asked if I could see it. It took her a while to realize that I was asking to see her breast. Once she realized she took off her shirt. I leaned over and started licking her nipples. After a few seconds she asked

"Is it OK if we stop?"

"Sure. Do you want me to lick your pussy?"

"No thanks. I appreciate the offer though."

I think she may have said something about her being in a relationship but I don't remember. What I do remember is me not wanting to go home. I spent the night lying next to her thinking nothing in particular. I woke up the next morning and took the bus to work. Through the years I've spoken to her a few times online but I never saw her again.

...

What Have we Learned?

When I first started writing this chapter I had maybe 3 or 4 stories in my head. Then I started writing and the number of stories started to balloon and I was dumbfounded by just how terrible I was at this. Clearly I knew I was a failure but learning I was a colossal failure was pretty devastating. My biggest mistake was thinking that by dating different types of people I would eventually strike gold. Obviously this started in junior high when I was taunted for liking a "fat girl".

The running thread through all these stories is that I was always uncomfortable with myself. I always felt like I was missing something and that this other person was the final piece that would put my life where it needed to be. But people aren't puzzle pieces that you need to arrange and I know it's really easy to see this in hindsight but it's something that really needs to be said.

I think people feel this way because falling in love seems so universal. Not everyone will run a Fortune 500 company or run a marathon or successfully run for mayor but everyone gets a run at love, right? It's the part of life that we all get to share so if I can't even do that then there must be something wrong with me.

This fear first started when my best friend from junior high told me how he lost his virginity. I called him a liar to his face but I knew he wasn't. Everyone knew that he was cooler than me. There was no need for him to make up stories. After that everyone around me started getting girls' phone numbers and the fear grew bigger and bigger as the years past: "No one is ever going to like me." I don't need to tell you how I took it when my friends started getting girlfriends.

I wish I could say that this fear went away or that I conquered it with sheer willpower but I didn't. I got lucky. After years of disappointment I met someone I liked who liked me back and it worked. I didn't wait patiently. I worried about it

constantly. I needed to know why no one liked me and then

one day someone did. And that was that.

Chapter 10: Failing at Travel

For a person that's lived most of his life in large cities I've been stranded in the middle of nowhere quite a few times. Sometimes my ride broke down, sometimes it ran out of gas but most of the time I just didn't have a car. Once I took a bus from Woodland Hills to Irvine (a 70 mile distance) to see N.E.R.D. perform. The concert was over at about midnight and by then there were no more buses that could take me home. I ended up sleeping in the bathroom stall of the train station because it was too cold to spend the night outside. I got home at about 11:30AM. The point is that there have been several times in my life where it was extremely difficult for me to get from point A to point B.

Also, this was in 2006 when the Neptunes were still making music together. N.E.R.D.s' first album "In Search of ..." is a classic and I will fight anyone who says differently. However, their follow up albums are mostly garbage. This is probably because while Pharrell and Chad produced and programmed all the music, Spymob played all the instruments. I have no idea what Shay did. My guess is that he was the "Jarobi" of the group. For whatever reason Spymob didn't show up on subsequent albums, which lead everything afterwards to sound like dog shit. That night I also got to see The Roots, Talib Kweli, Skillz (formerly know as Mad Skillz), Robert Randolph and the Family Band, and Common so that 70-mile trek was totally worth it. But I digress. Here are some more travelling stories.

...

I've lived in Los Angeles since 2002 and I've never been pulled over in a car. I HAVE been pulled over on a bicycle... twice. The fist time it happened was at about 3am. I had been working the overnight shift at my job and was on my way home when this bright light hit the back of my head. I didn't know what was happening so I looked back at what appeared to be a tractor beam. From what I could tell there was a car riding in the turning lane going about 5 miles an hour or however fast the average person can ride a bike. They didn't tell me to pull over so we continued like this for about two blocks. Eventually one of the officers got on the horn and told me to stop peddling and put the bike on the ground. I did as I was told.

They got out of their car, hands on their guns, and asked me if I had any weapons on me. I made the mistake of putting my hands in my jacket pocket. I wasn't reaching for anything but it was cold and because it had been such a long time since I had been approached by a police officer I forgot the protocol of keeping my hands visible at all times. This was my first mistake. In my defense they never told me to put my hands up.

My second mistake was when I told them I didn't have a weapon. I worked in a warehouse so I pretty much always had a box cutter on me. After I acknowledged my mistake one of the officers told me to reach for it slowly, put it on the ground and kick it to him. After that they told me to put my hands behind my head and face the wall. I asked them for the first time what all this was about, neither one of them answered.

I've never understood why police officers do this. I've been stopped by police officers before and they have never told me why they are stopping me until the whole situation was over. I know plenty of people have the same story. Being stopped by the police and not being told why does not help assuage the situation. Having someone put his or her hands on me and not tell me why does not make me feel safe. It makes me feel like I need to defend myself.

During the search they retrieved my ID from my back pocket. Because I didn't drive or have a car I never bothered getting a California license. They looked at my Texas driver's license and asked me if it was my current address. After they frisked me and didn't find anything they asked me if I had any tattoos. They wrote them down and informed me that I fit a description of another man that was riding his bike with a revolver in his jacket pocket and robbing people. (FYI: this is far from the first time I've "fit a description.") While this was being explained to me another police car rolled by but they waved him off. Apparently they called for backup. Before they let me go they told me to stop riding my bike on the sidewalk.

This happened to me again in the exact same place about two weeks later. The only difference was that it happened at about 9pm. I guess it's my fault for wearing a hoodie.

...

In addition to being pulled over from time to time, living in LA without a car was especially stressful because when I was working in Hollywood I lived far far away in the San Fernando Valley. One night after a recording session I tried to take the bus home. I ended up getting on a southbound bus, which was the opposite direction I needed to go. When I tried to go back I got slapped with the reality that there were no more busses going north. I was stranded somewhere in West LA with no way to get home. I was scared but I was also angry. Why wasn't anything working out for me? Why couldn't I catch a break? Why was I being punished?

I walked to a pay phone to try and call a cab. As I stood by the phone a guy walked past me. He was a Black kid that looked to be about my age, weight, height and looked vaguely like me. He asked me if I could lend him a few dollars so he could get home. I looked at him with all the anger I could must and said, "Man, I'm stranded too. I'm trying to help myself!" He looked back at me in shock. Then he scrunched up his face to symbolize the international token for "–fuck's your problem?" Then he walked away.

I ended up getting a cab ride from Hollywood to Woodland Hills, which are about 20 miles apart. Before we took off the cab driver actually asked me if I was sure about taking a cab that far. I didn't have a choice; I had just moved to LA and I didn't know any other way to get home. The trip ended up costing me $60. When I got home I realized I didn't have my key and had to wait outside my apartment door for an hour before my roommate come home and let me in.

Of everything that happened that night the thing that I remember most vividly is yelling at the payphone guy. He was just a guy trying to get home. Just like me. Although he had the same frame as me I'm not 100% sure he actually looked like me. That's probably my memory tricking me into treating this like the metaphor that it isn't. If I believed in that kind of thing I would say that this was a lesson in the universality of human suffering. We all just need to "walk in other peoples shoes" and be more companionate to each other. But this is all hogwash. The truth is I was a jerk who was focusing too much on his own discomfort to realize that I wasn't the only person in the world. I was taking my anger out on someone who didn't deserve it. I wish I could tell you I learned this lesson and never did anything like that again. But any woman I've been in a relationship with will tell you otherwise.

Eventually I learned how to get around LA using the metro but after about 12am most busses stopped running. This posed a problem because most nights I didn't leave the recording studio until 1am. This meant that I would usually have to take a cab to the closest bus stop that was still in service and walk 6 blocks home. One time while standing on

Hollywood and Highland (a very popular intersection in Hollywood) I called a cab from a payphone. During the day there where usually cabs up and down the block but it was 2am and the streets were empty. I stood on the corner and waited for about 5 minutes before I saw a cab approaching. He got about 30 feet away from me before he stopped in the middle of the street and made a U-turn. I looked behind me to see if there was an axe murderer, flowing lava, a pack of wild bees or some other monstrosity lurking behind me. Nothing. I stood on the corner for a few seconds and thought about why the cabdriver would turn around so abrupt... oh. I'm a Black man standing on the corner at 2am.

This reminded me of when I first got to LA and was living in Inglewood. The cabdriver asked me to pay in advance. I had only been in a cab about 2 other times in my life but I could tell from watching TV and movies that this wasn't normal. Still, at least this driver stopped the car and let me in. This guy busted a u-ey as if I didn't see him. As if he weren't *literally* the only car driving on the street. Lucky for me there was a cab parked not to far away that had just finished his lunch break. After he switched his "Off Duty" light I yelled across the street to see if he could take me to Studio City. I half expected him to give me an excuse but he smiled agreeingly and told me to hop in.

...

People tend to have 2 very different views of the American South. Most people who have never been view it as the most backward part of America. Typically after they've been their opinion is that southerners are surprisingly friendly. I'm sure the same can be said about North Korea.

I don't believe in the dichotomy of the American South: that it is either violently racist or cloyingly sweet. My feeling is that southerners tend to be more candid. For better or worse you always know where they stand. Unfortunately, you may not always know where *you* stand.

Case in point the only time I was stopped on a trip from Texas to Florida was in Alabama. I was on the highway in the middle of the night and a car sped pass me going 90. Tiny red and blue lights immediately started flashing behind me and shortly after I saw the brake lights of the speeding car. As the cop car got closer I eased off the gas petal. My car could barely go the speed limit so this meant that I was now driving about 50 mph. The Police car zoomed ahead of me about 10 feet and then started to slow down. At this point I was not panicking. He eventually slowed down enough to pull up behind me. *Now* I was panicking. He pulled me over, asked me to get out of the car and informed me that I had a broken brake light. He was correct... kind of. The *cover* of my brake light cracked 3 months prior and created a golf ball-sized hole. I placed translucent red tape over the hole and called it a day. The *light* worked perfectly. It worked so perfectly that no police officer in Texas, Louisiana, or Mississippi had pulled me over in the last 3 months. But this was Alabama. After I told him that I would get the light fixed he asked me if he could search my car. I was moving at the time so my car was packed to the hilt with everything I owned in the world.

So let's recap: I'm in Alabama, in the middle of the night, on the side of the road, with no witnesses and a police officer that pulled over the slower of two moving cars.

"So, you want me to take all my stuff out of my car?"

"In order to search it, yes, I need to take everything out of your car."

"Sure, whatever."

"I'm going to need a 'Yes' or 'No' from you."

"Yes."

He walked over to the car, peeked in for a few seconds and told me I was free to go. I knew where this guy stood. He was a bully. Maybe it was fueled by racism, maybe it was laziness but in the end he was just a guy that wanted to see if he could make me do what he wanted. I on the other hand had no idea where I stood with this guy. What I do know is that I thought about this incident way more times than he ever did.

...

Traveling has also given me ample opportunities to be yelled at. It's the mixture of ignorance and vulnerability that makes being yelled at while you're traveling just a tad bit more humiliating than being yelled at by your parents or your girl/boy friend. This first time I remember being yelled at while traveling was on my senior trip to the East coast. We spent time in Washington DC, Philadelphia, Baltimore, and of course New York City. We were all going into a building somewhere in Manhattan that had a revolving door. I don't know for sure that I was in Manhattan but it was a fancy building that had a revolving door so where else could I have been? Anyway I was somehow the last one of my class to go inside. This was possibly because I had never actually used a revolving door before. As I was about to go in a businessman walked in front of me as I was getting up my courage to walk through. He already had his hand on the door but because I was standing there first I assumed I should be the first to go in. The businessman stopped dead in his tracks. He understandable thought I was trying to share his partition and he was having none of it. In my memory he was 10 feet tall so he had to bend down to look me in my eye, wag his finger in my face and yell at me "One at a time!" His voice sounded like all of New York telling me I needed to go back to Nowhere East Texas and ride a cow or whatever it was we did there. I literally wanted to cry but somehow I didn't. I went into the building, joined my group and never told them about what happened.

A couple of hours later I was kicked out of a bodega for spending too much time in the magazine section. An Asian man yelled at me in the most stereotypical way possible that "You no read! You buy!" Apparently New York was just as mean and inhospitable as it was portrayed to be in the movies. Go figure. I was so scared that it would be 13 years until I would step foot in that city again.

Years later while on a trip to Egypt I ended up with an 8-hour overnight layover in Germany. As much as I hate to generalize an entire country by its airport I have to say that my time in that country was filled with a wealth of stereotypically cold German behavior. The most uncongenial moment was when I wasn't sure where the terminal was for my next flight and I decided to ask someone who worked at the airport. I looked for a place that wasn't too congested but still had signs of life. I spotted an area around a corner that looked like it would be a good place to ask a question without cutting in line or interrupting the flow of work. The desk wasn't blocked off; I didn't hop over any yellow tape to get there but in all farness it did look like it was a place that may have been designated for employees only. As I approached the desk smiling and with my palms raised to show that I came in peace two German ladies that had been previously talking to each other spotted me and simultaneously let out a scream like Donald Sutherland from Invasion of the Body Snatchers. To this day I don't remember if they yelled at me in German or English but it was apparent I wasn't supposed to be there and they were incredibly displeased. This was the last time I remember being so shocked, scared and confused all at the same time. I was so discombobulated that I walked back around the corner and spent the next 7 hours sleeping on a bench until it was time for me to find my terminal. I haven't been back to Germany since.

...

When I was 22 I rented a moving truck for the first time. All the other times I had moved I could fit everything in the back seat of my car. For the first time in my life I had furniture.

I assumed renting a moving truck was like renting a car and although I had never done that either I did know that you had to use a credit card. Because I didn't have a card or a checking account I sent my parents the money and asked if they could rent the truck for me online.

When I got to the rental place and found out that none of that was necessary I was heartbroken. Not only did I not need a credit card but I also could have paid cash. This wouldn't have been as big of a problem if I hadn't sent almost all my money to my parents to rent the truck for me. This same weekend my parents were at a Christian retreat in Corpus Christi, TX and they really didn't have the time or desire to take care of my transportation issues. They had paid $300 for this weekend and had no intentions of missing out. Luckily my grandmother intervened and convinced my dad to have his credit union wire me the money. Somehow my mother didn't give the credit union a destination city (the credit union didn't ask for one either) and they were unable to send the money and because my parents were at the retreat and didn't pick up their cell phones the credit union couldn't reach them to ask for another city. By the time I found all this out and called the credit union it was too late. They couldn't send money after 4 pm and they weren't able to until Monday morning. This was all happening on a Friday. What made this situation even worse was that my lease had expired at the end of the month and it was now the 5th. Given everything else that had gone wrong I wouldn't have been surprised if my landlord had locked me out so I made it a point to leave the apartment as little as possible until the coast was clear.

Gladly nothing ever happened and eventually I got a moving truck. I rented it for 10 days. If I could get from Florida to California in 4 days I would have about 6 days to find an apartment. If I couldn't pull that off I would end up living in a

storage facility amongst my lumpy futon and CD collection.

Luckily I found some roommates.

Chapter 11: Failing at Roommates

Before we begin I just want to let you know that there are a lot of names to keep up with in this chapter. To limit the confusion I've inserted headings to let you know where we are in the roommate rotation.

Me, my cousins' ex-fiancés' mother, my cousins' ex-fiancés' sister, my cousins' ex-fiancés' brother-in-law, and my cousins' ex-fiancés' niece

Before leaving Orlando I called someone that had a room for rent in LA and told them I would be there in 2 days. The first day I drove non-stop from Orlando to Houston. I spent the night on a friends couch and left the next morning. I drove the next day from Houston to Phoenix where I met up with my older cousin. There I made a call to the person that was renting out a room only to find that he already gave it to someone else. Because I had never looked for a roommate before I was surprised that he didn't save the room for me even though I said that I wanted it. Some people.

When my cousin heard that I was moving to LA without a place to stay he decided to make the journey to Los Angeles with me. It was where his ex-fiancé lived and he figured that she could put me up for a few days until I got things sorted. I ended up staying with my cousins' ex-fiancés' mother in Inglewood. The only thing they had for me to sleep on was a creaky daybed built for an eight-year-old girl. I looked like Carroll Barker on the set of *Baby Doll*.

I spent most of my days looking for apartments on their computer that was fully equipped with a noisy dial-up modem. When I wasn't looking for apartments I sat in the living room watching the news because it was the only daytime TV I could watch without feeling like my brain was melting. One day a woman whom I assume was my cousins' ex-fiancés' sister invited her boyfriend (babies father? husband?) over. They went into her bedroom, which was inches away from the living room couch and left the door open. A child whom I assume was her daughter sat on the couch next to me. I'm not good with children's ages but she looked about 3 years old. After a few minutes she called the 3 year old into the room and shut the door. Within the next few seconds all I heard was hard-core fucking for a solid 10 minutes. When it was over my cousins' ex-fiancés' sister walked out of the room to the kitchen to get a glass of water followed by her daughter. They walked back to the room leaving the door open. I walked back to my room and started looking for apartments.

I found an apartment in the north end of the San Fernando Valley in Woodland Hills. It was, in ever sense of the word, far removed from Inglewood and nowhere near the recording studio in Hollywood where I would be working. It was a three-bedroom apartment where 3 guys already lived and I had to share the master bedroom with one of them. It cost $400 a month and I had no other options so I agreed. Because my only mode of transportation was the moving truck that I needed to return the next day, I moved in 10 minutes after I looked that place.

Me, Jacob, Peter and Charles

I shared the master bedroom with Jacob. We got along pretty well and to this day he is still one of my best friends. Peter had his own room on the opposite end of the apartment. He was a tolerable roommate as long as he took his medication. Off his meds he had the tendency to hump people. He was also a devout Christian. I'm not sure which one of those things I found more annoying. Charles was an aspiring actor that moved to LA from South Carolina. Within minutes of me moving in he asked me if it was true that all Black people could dance. He would later ask me why all Black women seemed to love Denzel Washington. For obvious reasons I never liked Charles much but sometimes I felt bad for him because he always genuinely wanted to know the answer. His racism wasn't driven by hate so much as ignorance. I know those things aren't mutually exclusive but with him they seemed to be.

It was with this group of guys that I watched the debut of Chappelle's Show. In case you don't remember the first episode introduced the world to Clayton Bigsby; the Black White supremacist that didn't know that he was Black because he was also blind. As the sketch progressed Clayton spewed racial epitaphs that I found hard to laugh at in my current company. My new roommates didn't have that problem. When Clayton talked about Black people with their big noses "breathing up all the White mans air" they doubled over with laughter. When Dave Chappelle later left his show because he felt people were laughing for the wrong reasons I knew exactly what he meant. FYI: After further review I came to love the Clayton Bigsby sketch and think it was one of the funnies things ever allowed on TV.

In order to financially support his acting dream Charles became a bouncer at a bar a few miles up the road. He wasn't particular good at either profession. I never recall him booking a gig and he was always covered in bruises. One night he asked if I wanted to get a few drinks with him at his bar. I questioned why he wanted to go to his workplace on his day off. He responded by telling me how much everyone loved him there.

Because I didn't have anything better to do I agreed to go with him. His coworkers seemed like nice enough people but none of them appeared to be his friend. Almost Immediately and totally unprovoked Charles started knocking back shots of whiskey and within the hour he started taking swings at anyone that walked by including his "friends". After he got out of control his fellow bouncers tossed him head first into the car with his feet twisted around the headrest. He then proceeded to vomit on his floor mats. They gave me his keys and I drove us back home. I pulled him out of his car, up into the elevator and into his bed all the while wondering why I was doing this much work for a person I could barely stand. I cursed my parents for raising me this way. Not long after this incident Charles realized that his acting dream would never come true and moved back to South Carolina.

Me, Jacob, Peter, Sean and Benny

After Charles came Benny. Although he tended to have unnervingly loud sex with his girlfriend he was pretty easy to get along with. At this time we also had a kid sleeping on our couch named Sean. Peter, unbeknownst to us, invited him and I assume he was off his medication when he did. Sean was younger than all of us and had an even younger girlfriend who seemed to only watch the TV show Friends when she came over. The only thing I recall him owning was a George Forman Grill with which he exclusively cooked extra-rare steaks washed down with an extra large protein shake. Other than the night he uncharacteristically started blaring 'In Da Club' at 4 am he didn't cause much trouble. One day I woke up and didn't see him lying on the couch and I knew are time together had ended. He left his George Forman Grill though.

176

Me, Jacob, Peter and Martin

About the same time Sean disappeared Benny decided to move out and was replaced by Martin. Everyone got along pretty well with Martin but he didn't get along too well with Peter. It seems Martin had been humped one too many times. Lucky for Martin, Peter moved out soon after he moved in. Peter felt he was being ridiculed for his religious beliefs and felt it would be better for him to live somewhere where his Christianity wouldn't be mocked. None of us had any idea what he was talking about and collectively did nothing to dissuade him.

Me, Jacob, Chris and Martin

I remember almost nothing about Chris other than when we moved in we gained a big screen TV. He was also a minor player in the following story:

One Saturday night the boys of Apartment 317 decided to throw a party. We cleaned the house and invited the few friends we had. The only problem was that we couldn't scare up any girls. Undeterred we decided to go through with everything as planed. Although none of us had ever seen Field of Dreams we felt that if we threw it, they would come. A little before the festivities where to begin Martin and Chris decided to go to the store to get ice. About 30 minutes later they came back with 6 sorority sisters that where looking for a good time. I don't remember if they bought ice. We embraced our good fortune, turned on some music and started pouring drinks. The girls were smart enough to let us do the lion's share of the drinking.

I was sitting down talking to one of the sisters when Martin sauntered over and informed her that I was a rapper. She gave a minimal amount of acknowledgment and Martin took this as a slight. He leaned over to me and in a voice that he though was a whisper and said "Don't worry man, she's a bitch anyway." If this where a teen comedy set in the late nineties the record scratch would have been placed right about there. It seemed that all 6 girls heard this at the same time, stood up and marched towards the door. None of us had the sea legs to try and turn this around so we just stood there clutching our red plastic cups and tried to remember a time about 2 minutes ago when we were kings.

I walked across the room to turn off the music and before I reached the space bar Martin, probably because he realized what he had just done, threw up on the living room floor. Seconds later Jacob threw up in the middle of our bedroom. That was officially the end of the night. I don't remember what Chris did but he probably threw up too. I resisted the urge to vomit and went to bed to dream of what could have been. We all woke up the next morning and never spoke of the incident again. Shortly thereafter, Mike replaced Chris.

Me, Jacob, Mike and Martin

Mike was a musician. Because it was the early 2000s he was in a Screamo band and because of that he constantly had a trail of women leading to his bedroom. Every week I would see him with a new starry-eyed, tattooed, dark-haired, vampire girl. The weird thing was that he seemed to be deeply in love with every single one of them. He wasn't "emo" in the trendy sense of the word. He really was emotional. It wasn't just song lyrics with him: every Friday **he was in love**. He was the only one that could ever get drugs and girls to any of our parties so we were sad when he told us he was leaving. What made this even worse was when Jacob said he was moving out too. By this time Jacob and I had shared the master bedroom for 4 years. Not only was I loosing a dear friend but now we had to replace two roommates at once. We decided it would be easier to occupy the master bedroom so I moved to my own room on the other side of the apartment.

Me, the Bear, the Pixie and Martin

We ended up getting a couple to move in that I shall refer to as the Bear and the Pixie. The Bear was a few years older than the Pixie and I got the sense that that was why the Pixie liked him. She seemed to be dating him because it pissed off her mother and the Bear was just happy to be wanted. At any rate they were pretty nice people who also came with an astonishingly well-trained collie. The problem came when The Bear and The Pixie realized that mutual distain of someone's mother does not a stable relationship make. The Bear could only pretend to enjoy raves and electronic music for so long before he started to show his teeth. This was bad news for the both of them but more importantly it was bad news for Martin and me. Before long we were back to looking for a new roommate.

Me, Dave and Martin

Dave was handsome (mix-raced), smart (Princeton), confident (see aforementioned attributes), and younger than both of us. He was also willing to pay what we were asking so the three of us hit it off instantly. The fact that Dave wasn't the Lothario that Martin and me thought he was didn't stop us from following him into nightclubs. We always came home alone but our spirits where never dampened. We would always have a great time while we where out and then go home to our respective rooms and masturbate the loneliness away.

It wasn't until Dave moved out that we realized that he was a complete stranger to us. We didn't know where he worked or how he got this money. We didn't know where he was from. We didn't even really know why he was moving out. All we knew was that one day he told us that it was time for him to go and then he left. We didn't even know where he was moving. And even though he left the apartment we still saw him a couple times a week. Especially when we got our new roommate.

Me, Phat Zane and Martin

I never got a chance to interview Dave's replacement. All I knew about him was that he was a Canadian that moved down here for work. It wasn't until he paid us two month's rent on the day he moved in that he let us in on his little secret: he was a porn actor. His name was Phat Zane. He had won a few awards in Canada and now he felt it was time for him to step up to the big leagues. None of us had more questions than Dave:

"Whom have you worked with?"

"What's the secret to a huge load?"

"Why do they call it the 'money shot'?"

"Does everyone really have Herpes?"

We fantasized about all the porn parties we were going to be invited to.

All things considered Zane was pretty normal. He didn't spend money on anything other than medicinal weed and candy. He didn't keep anything in his room other than the mattress that Dave left behind and his big screen TV. And we only hung out with his porn friends once.

Me, Zane, Martin, and Dave met up with them downtown at a bar. None of them where particularly hot but that's not necessarily a prerequisite for porn-stardom. They looked like teenage girls that matured sooner than the other girls and decided to take advantage of it. To their credit none of them seemed like victims but they certainly seemed oblivious to the fact that they didn't have as many options as they thought they had. They all had a look in their eyes that suggest that they still had not come to grips with the reality that what they were doing was pretty weird. That's the difference between an amateur and a professional. A professional fully accepts what they are doing is weird and even embraces it. Armatures have to fake it until they make. And if they don't make it, that's a long walk back home.

We hung out with them for a while, had a few beers and eventually they asked use if we wanted to go back to their place. "Yes, please." They lived in a nice house in San Fernando Valley (of course) with 3 other actors. None of us were expecting playboy bunnies to be running around topless but this place looked like a shelter for runaway teens that was run by other runaway teens. It was somewhere between Party of 5 and Lord of the Flies. There was a coffee table adorned with bong resin and a wireless router, a kitchen table stacked with empty pizza boxes and a bathroom with a curious amount of hand sanitizer. One girl walked around in her pajamas and Ugg boots talking on the phone to a person she later said was her boyfriend. I couldn't help but wonder what he must be like. Was he back in Wisconsin asking her what her classes were like at UCLA? Or was he also an actor jealous of her success?

We didn't hang out there long. I don't even recall sitting down. After we left we went to Denny's and had breakfast. We didn't get home until sunrise. The next time I tell this story it will go a little more like this: we went out and had drinks with a few porn stars and the guy that dresses up as Superman on Hollywood Blvd. (this part is actually true), went back to their place and came home when the sun came up. The End.

At any rate that was the first and last time we hung out with Phat Zane with or without his friends. As the months passed Zane became more reclusive. It seemed as though all he did was hang out in his room smoke weed and play videogames. That was all fine and well but he was also a little late on his bills. He promised us by the first he would have everything in order and we had no choice but to take his word.

On New Year's Eve Martins' brother invited us to his house. Neither one of us had anything planned so we agreed and seeing as it was New Years Eve and he also seemed a little down the past few weeks we asked Zane if he wanted to come with us. He told us that he was just going to stay home and we both felt a little sorry for him.

We spent the night in the corner of a stranger's house (Martin was not very close with his brother) watching other strangers 10 years our senior dance to Kanye West. When we came home all we could hear was Zane's big screen TV blaring. After we went to bed we woke up to the same blaring TV. We opened the door to find that Zane was gone. Apparently Zane hadn't had any gigs in a while and ran out of money. He owed us about $1500 for rent and utilities. I would like to take this time to let you know that all the names in this book are fake except for Phat Zane... cause fuck that guy.

Me, Derrick and Martin

Derrick had two jobs and he usually paid for everything in cash. By this time Martin and I were hemorrhaging money so we weren't too picky when it came to a roommate. In hindsight that was another risky move. If a person has more than one job they're not making very much money. And if they don't have a checking account all bets are off. (Side note: I am truly grateful my original roommates didn't follow these guidelines.)

After a few months we found out that Derrick was a serious alcoholic. The first sign was when I went to get a shot of vodka from a bottle I kept on the kitchen counter and discover that it had been emptied and refilled with water. I checked my other bottles and found that they were empty too. When I confronted him he promised me that he would replace them. What worried me the most was that those bottles were practically full the day before.

Things went downhill from there. Every few days he would drag out trash bags full of empty bottles. Before long he lost both of his jobs and Martin and I had a sit-down to figure out what we were going to do. We tried to confront Derrick but we ended up getting the same excuses as before. He even tried showing us pictures of his kid. On the one hand he was clearly a person in need of help. He literally couldn't stop drinking on his own but neither one of us knew him well enough to genuinely want to help him. It sounds harsh but what we wanted was our rent paid. After the incident with Zane it was hard to be optimistic. We knew it was a matter of time before he would disappear.

Me and Martin

On that front Derrick did not disappoint. One day we can home to his empty bedroom with two bowling ball sized holes in the wall that completely erased any notion of us getting our deposit back. We panicked. As far as we could tell we had three options: 1) We could try our luck with another roommate, 2) we could move out, or 3) we could move into a smaller apartment in the same building. All of these options had some pretty heavy downsides: 1) financially we couldn't take the hit of another roommate disappearing, 2) if one of us moved out we would leave the other one with a huge apartment they couldn't afford and if we moved out together we would have to pay for breaking the lease, and 3) we would end up paying more in rent because we would have to split it 2 ways instead of 3 or 4. Out of loyalty to each other we ended up moving into a two-bedroom apartment in the same building to avoid breaking the lease. We both had to adjust our budgets but in the end everything worked out and when our lease was up a year later we parted ways.

When it was all said and done I ended up staying in that apartment building for 8 years. I only lived in the house I grew up in for 7. Sometimes I wonder why I stayed. To everyone else that apartment was just a stop on the way to something else. To me it was home. I moved out of Tyler, Texas when I was 19 with no thoughts of moving back. I always felt that me moving back would mean I was losing ground. I spent most of my time in that apartment building trying to hold on. I spent so much time doing that I never really moved forward. I had no real goals so I had nothing to aim for.

I spent a lot of time there but I would never say I wasted my time. You can only waste your time if you are supposed to be doing something else. And you can only do something if you know what it is you want. It took me a long time to figure

out what I wanted.

Chapter 12: Failing at Employment

Every year when my sister had a ballet recital my parents, like many other parents, helped with the production. My mom would help the girls with their makeup and my dad would help building sets. Most years I would just stand to the side and wait for the whole thing to be over. But one year I helped my dad with the sets and on opening night I was in charge of the curtain.

The director of the ballet school was Mrs. Gina St Michaels. Her students feared and loved her in that order. She was also a teacher at my junior high but I never had any classes with her. During rehearsal my curtain skills were on point. I never missed a cue and I could always open the curtain with what appeared to be one smooth motion. No herkin'. No jerkin'. To be honest the job was pretty easy. Mrs. St Michaels, who was sitting 3 feet away from me, would say "curtain" and I would open the curtain. The job was pretty hard to screw up. That opening night I learned something about myself: the world hasn't created a job yet that I can't screw up.

When the lights went down and the show started I realized that during rehearsal it was never this dark backstage. During the rehearsal I could always see Mrs. St Michaels standing 3 feet away from me. I didn't realize it until then but I always depended on her head nod to tell me what to do. Now I couldn't see my hand in front of my face. As soon as the first number ended and the applause died down all I could hear in my mind was "curtain...curtain...curtain." I couldn't decipher Mrs. St Michaels "curtain" from the voices in my head. This went on for about an hour until I heard the actual cue and closed the curtain before intermission.

This should have been a time for me to gather my thoughts but it immediately dawned on me that I would have to open the curtain again pretty soon. I realized then that this was way too much responsibility for a 14 year old. After about 15 minutes the voice in my head started up again and before I knew it I was pulling the curtain open.

"What are you doing? Now I have to reset the lights!"

I started to close the curtain.

"No, leave it open."

The curtain was left half open for the remainder of the intermission. I expected Mrs. St Michaels to wring my neck but she never did. She handled the entire situation like the professional she was and presumably still is. She continued directing her crew and when it was time she said "curtain" and I opened the curtain the rest of the way. The voices didn't disappear but somehow I got through it without any other incidents. No one ever said a word about my monumental blunder. The crisis in my head was just that: in my head. This experience would mirror my relationships with various employment opportunities for the remainder of my life.

...

For most of his adult life my grandfather worked for a concrete company. My father said that as a young man he had never seen his father-in-law without a pair of work boots on. When my grandfather wasn't making and/or delivering bricks (I really don't know which one he did) he would come home to his private wood business. When he retired in his 60s he delivered wood fulltime. Early in the morning he and whoever agreed to work with him would go out to the woods and help him cut down a tree. Once the tree was on the ground he would cut the tree up into 2-foot long logs. He would use a wedge and an axe for the larger logs and load them on his truck. For the smaller logs he would use his gas powered wood splitter before loading it onto his truck. He would then drive that truck home and begin unloading it in his yard where he kept his product until a customer asked for a delivery. Anyone who worked with him did not go home until well after sundown.

When I was 13 my first job was to remove the brush after he cut down the tree so he could cut the branches into logs. By the time I was 14 I could properly stack a cord of wood. By the time I was 15 I could use the wood splitter, and split a log with an axe. When I was 16 I could drive the tractor that was used to move the heavier tree trunks. When I turned 17 I got the fuck out of the wood business.

One day with my grandfather and you would defiantly know what a day's work feels like. Four years would hold you for a lifetime. One thing you would not learn from working with my grandfather is how much a regular person gets paid. When I was younger he would give me about $20 for a days work. My rate increased, as I got older. For all the 12-hour days I worked he never gave me over $40 at the end of the day. That's $3.33 an hour if you're keeping score. This was part of the reason for my quick departure. The other reason was that I had no interest in chopping wood.

I was the youngest of all my family members that worked with him and when they had enough of hauling wood they moved on. Although my grandfather still had a few good years left in him he was getting a little long in the tooth and was looking for a successor. He had 5 kids and all of them girls. I'm sure some part of him resented that. All of his older grandkids had left to start other jobs. His other grandkids were too young to try to teach. I was just the right age. I hated to let him down but there was no way I was the man he was looking for. So, like all my other family, as soon as I could I found a regular job I split.

My first job outside the wood business was at a Christian summer camp. It was also a summer camp I went to as a teenager. As a kid I had a pretty good time there. There was the one afternoon that I came back to my bunk to hear my lily-white bunkmates having a discussion about the word "Nigger". They discussed how even though they hated the word it was obvious that niggers existed and they ruined everything. This was years before Chris Rock would mine this same premise for comedy gold on *Bring the Pain*. Luckily one of the guys there was also my classmate, vouched for me and asserted that I wasn't a nigger. I sat quietly on my top bunk and waited for the discussion to be over. Sadly, this wouldn't be the last time I would sit quietly while a room full of my white peers tossed around the word nigger in such a cavalier manner. Aside for this everything else at summer camp went swimmingly.

Years later when I applied for the job I was too young to be a counselor so I worked in the kitchen with all the other youngsters. Everyone on staff had the pleasure of receiving a "camp name". The ceremony was the same for everyone. You sat on a stool in front of the rest of the staff, one person would ask you questions, and the rest of the staff would shout out potential names. Most often a person received their name because of an embarrassing story. The names were meant to be a conversation starter with the campers. Because I didn't want to get stuck with a silly name I chose to give them as little to work with as possible and decided to only give one-word answers. It just so happened that all the answers to the questions they asked me were "Yes" and I was thereafter known as "Yes-Man".

There was only one other naming session that I remember. It was a naming session in which one of the staff shouted out "tar baby". I don't remember why that name was yelled out but I do remember everyone else's reaction being cheers and applause. I didn't know what to do so I stood up and looked directly at the person at the front of the room holding the microphone. After a few seconds the room fell silent and I pleaded "Tar baby?" No one said a word for a few seconds and I sat back down. After a few seconds they moved on with the naming session. Only one person spoke to me about that day at it was the guy holding the microphone. Days later he came up to me and let me know that he didn't mean any offence. I don't remember my response but knowing me I probably told him that everything was OK.

Moments like that have always been the hardest for me. Was I overreacting or just reacting? Was I standing up for something or just reinforcing the "angry-black-guy" stereotype? Did anything I did make any difference at all? Throughout the summer there were a few more incidents where I had to ask myself those questions like when the only other black staff member began singing "Killing Me Softly" and others asked me to join in assuming I knew all the words and more importantly that I was a great singer. Other than incidents like that it was a great summer.

I worked in the kitchen preparing food and washing dishes. Once a week we would perform skits during dinner but that was the only real interaction we had with the campers. Most of the kitchen help was only hired for one month at a time but because I enjoyed the work and I lived close by they asked me to stay the whole summer. I was the only one they asked to do this so I felt pretty special. After the summer was over I even worked on the weekends. The following year when I applied for a camp counselor position I was denied. Everyone I talked to about it seemed utterly surprised that I wasn't hired but their opposition didn't seem to make a difference. Maybe if I had let them rename me Tar Baby.

When the summer was over I had my first real job interview at Wal-Mart. My dad taught me how to fill out a job application and helped me get the interview. The one thing he didn't prepare me for was the pre-hire questionnaire. It was one of those questionnaires that asked questions like "If you saw someone steal a quarter would you report it?" & "Do you know anyone that does drugs?" Not knowing any better I answered everything honestly. When my interviewer entered the room to go over the questionnaire with me the first thing he did after he sat down was let out a long sigh. He told me that there were no "right" or "wrong" answers but well… my answers were wrong.

He explained to me in the most indirect way possible that if I wanted a job I was going to have to tell people what they wanted to hear. I couldn't believe that I was 17 and no one had ever told me that. It was my first lesson in politics. No one cares what you think. They only care that you know what you should think and that what you think you should think is also what they think you should think.

Obviously I didn't get the job but I learned a valuable lesion. Since then I've been given some variation of that same test everywhere I've ever applied and I've passed with flying colors. If anyone ever asks I've never met anyone that has ever seen illegal drugs and I spend my free time ratting out people who graze the mixed nuts at the supermarket. Scouts honor. (Full disclosure: I was never a Boy Scout. I never made it past Weebelow.)

My first actual job was at a thrift store. I worked there for about 2 weeks. I don't even remember getting a paycheck. I do remember the day I quit. I had prepared a speech to relay that I appreciated the opportunity but it was time for me to move on. Before I finished stumbling through the first sentence my boss asked me if I was quitting. I tripped over a few more words before my boss lost his patience. "If you're quitting had over your apron. I'm busy. I really don't have time for this." I handed over my apron and that was that. I tried to thank him but he left me alone in his office before I could finish.

There was really nothing wrong with the job. I just wasn't happy. For some reason I thought a job would be fun or at the very least it would be interesting. The thrift store was none of those things. I thought that doing something other than chopping wood would be an entrance into a new life for me. In truth working with my grandfather had spoiled me.

Sure, it was tough work, but at the end of the day you had something to show for it. I mean you cut down a fucking tree! No two trees where alike so every day you had the opportunity to learn something new. All I did at the thrift store was sweep floors and floors don't change much from day to day.

This was my second lesson in employment: jobs suck. It didn't matter which one I had, it would always be either a back breaking and/or soul sucking experience. That was why my next job was at Taco Bell. The fact that they paid me fifty cents more was an added bonus. I stayed there for 2 years. And what a two years it was. I worked the morning shift with Mexican gangbangers, was constantly sexually harassed by my stereotypical heavyset black female boss, had my first French kiss in the parking lot, was indirectly sprayed with mace, had my first direct interaction with a gay man, and simultaneously held down the drive-through and the front counter while my manager had a miscarriage in the women's bathroom. Alas, 2 years of coming home reeking of taco meat took its toll and I finally quit.

I quit to get a job at a telemarketing company that was hiring every 18-21 year old in town. Sure this job combined two things that I hate (talking on the phone and selling things) but they paid better than Taco Ball and I could wear my own clothes. As far as I know we weren't doing anything illegal but I certainly wouldn't have bought anything that I was selling. We called small business owners and ask them if they wanted a website designed for them. Because my company didn't design websites we would then connect them to a third party that would create their website. I had no idea who the third party was, what their websites looked like or if they were even real but if a person agreed I would get $2 dollars added to my paycheck. Some people loved it but for me doing this for 8 hours a day was torture.

Eventually the combination of hiring everyone that walked through the door and not having any new call list caused the company to cut back on hours. This led to a grand exodus to the brand new Wal-Mart Supercenter on the other side of town. Other than the store greeter I don't recall anyone over the age of 30 working with me at Wal-Mart. I assume most of us were hired because we were cheap labor. We didn't have mortgages to pay off and (most of us) didn't have children to feed. We didn't ask for a 401K and didn't care about health benefits. All we needed was gas money and that's exactly what they paid us. My time here was pretty uneventful. I worked there until I left for college.

My first year away at school, I worked at the Wal-Mart a few miles away from my school and came home the following summer. Before I tell you about working at a small town Wal-Mart I'll tell you about my last summer living with my parents. Since I had worked at the telemarketing company before I thought it would be easy for me to be rehired. I really didn't want to work there again but I needed the money.

I went into the office to get an application and they informed me that they could interview me as soon as I finished filling it out. I thought it was a little weird but I figured "Why not?" Moments after I handed my application over they called me into what appeared to be a makeshift office. The first question the interview asked me was if I applied there before. I replied "no". She noticed on my application that I said that I worked there before and she questioned me about it. I replied that I had worked there before but I thought she was asking if I had applied there recently. As in "had I applied there a few days ago?" She told me that the interview was over, stood up, and walked out the door. It all happen so fast I wasn't sure I understood what was happening. Had I really tanked an interview in under 60 seconds?

I'm not sure why I was so confused by her question but I *really* didn't understand why my answer caused such an angry response. This wasn't an interview for the FBI. They were telemarketers for gods' sake! They should be happy that *anyone* wanted the job.

For a number of reasons I was glad I never got hired: 1) a few months after I was rejected my friends who worked there started getting paychecks that bounced when they tried to cash them, 2) a few weeks after that the company closed down, & most importantly 3) literally no one wants to be a telemarketer.

I ended up working with my mom and my sister at a Christian bookstore. My mom had worked there for years. The "perks" were a never-ending supply of Christian T-Shits, books, videogames and music. Admittedly I'm playing a little fast and loose with the definition of "perks". The secret recipe of Christian commerce is to take a secular idea and add Jesus. Their slogan: "It doesn't have to be good, it just has to be Christian." It's a highly sustainable business model with not much room for growth. I could not in all honestly refer to receiving free Christian Rock CD's and cassettes a "perk".

Aside from the church we went to most of my families Christian interest spawned from this bookstore. The owner of the store had a son that attended the private school that my siblings and I eventually attended. It was also how my mom found out about the Christian Summer Camp that my sister and I attended and I later worked. The bookstore was also my sisters' first job. While I was toiling away in the woods with my grandfather she was stacking books. Now it was my turn to learn how the Bibles get engraved.

I could tell that the owner was simply doing my mom a favor by hiring me. That made things a little intense at times but for the most part everything went along fine. On the weekends I still worked with my grandfather because I felt like I owed it to him for leaving plus I wasn't in a position to turn down work. This would be the last summer my sister and me spent together before we disappeared from each other's lives. The same goes for my parents and me.

In the fall of 2000 I went back to school and got rehired at the Wal-Mart in Brenham, TX about 20 miles from where I lived. There was a Wal-Mart that was closer but they already had their fill of college students. The Wal-Mart in Brenham was much darker than the one I worked at back home. Here, people had families to feed. My coworkers weren't a gaggle of high school students looking for gas money. Practically every cashier was a single mother and every warehouse worker was a down-on-their-luck college dropout trying to make the best of things. It made me wonder what life had been like before Wal-Mart set up shop. I'm sure the denizens were excited at the prospect of new jobs and cheap merchandise. It would be a few years before their small businesses would shrivel up and their new jobs would pay them just enough to where the only place they could afford to shop for merchandise was Wal-Mart.

This is not to say that this was a sad place to work, far from it. Every weekend was like the lower deck of the Titanic. It turns out that life is pretty fun when you've never had anything and don't have anything to lose. I, unlike everyone else in town, had a lot to lose; namely my sanity. I had to get out of Brenham, TX so I got a second job at the Whataburger (not to be confused with What-A-Burger) across the parking lot. I worked at both places full time for 3 months before I almost died of exhaustion. Luckily I raised enough money to get out of Texas before I keeled over.

My next job was as a tour guide at my school in Orlando, FL. I would also call perspective students and answer any questions they may have. In the midst of this I developed a huge crush on my boss who looked like (to me anyway) a pregnant Salma Hayek.

The worst part of the job was when we called a perspective student and I had to talk down a parent that didn't want their child attending a trade school. Especially one that was as expensive as this. On the weekend I would usher hundreds of recent high school graduates and their parents through the many recording studios, post production suits, and computer labs the school had to offer. I never took a tour of the school before I came so it was fun to see it from this side. Sometimes for a little extra money I would provide private tours for the more discerning parents. All in all it was an OK job. It didn't pay much but then again we didn't do much. Also, because it didn't pay much most of my living expenses were paid for using my student loan money and because of that it's the only job I've ever had that I'm still paying for.

After my year was up in Florida I moved to California. After a month of looking for a job I finally got two. The first was at Restoration Hardware where I was paid $7.50 an hour to be a gift wrapper. The second was at Williams-Sonoma where I was paid $7 an hour to work in the warehouse. Each store was literally around the corner from each other in the same mall. I'm pretty sure that if they found out about each other I would have been fired for conflict of interest. After two weeks of Restoration Hardware I had to quit because I wasn't getting any hours. I only received one paycheck and that was for the two staff meetings I attended. I still needed money so I got a second warehouse job at the formerly defunct Circuit City where I was paid a whopping $7.75 an hour but after a few months I was making $10.25.

I really needed the job so during the interview I put on my best Jack McBrayer impersonation. I remember my boss being upset that I wasn't as loquacious as I had been in the interview. But what did he want from me? I was working in the warehouse.

My immediate supervisor was named Bob. He had been working in the back of that store for about 10 years and he no intentions of doing anything other than waiting on retirement. He was a hard worker. He didn't half-ass anything. He also wanted nothing to do with anything that went on in the front of the store. In other words he was like every warehouse worker you've ever met.

We were (mostly) lovable curmudgeons. The sales floor was a mix of Indian men in their forties who had families to support and White kids in their twenties who wanted to be actors/writers/musicians. The cashiers were mostly White girls in their twenties whose boyfriends were actors/writers/musicians and people of all ages who hadn't quite figured out what they were going to do with their lives. The managers were a pretty mixed bag but for the most part they were company men and women. Bob was not a company man. He wanted as little responsibility as possible. The higher ups also didn't want Bob to become a manager. Because he had been working there so long he was making about twice what I was making and only a little less than the store manager. Since making someone a manger would also include a 5% raise Bob would then be making about the same as or possibly more than the store manager. This is how I ended up becoming the warehouse manager. I was grateful for the raise, Bob didn't have to take on any unnecessary responsibility, and the management team didn't have to worry about a subordinate making more than them. Of course Bob was still the boss although he would never admit it. I was more or less Bob's liaison.

I liked working in a warehouse. There's not a lot of room for gray in the warehouse. If someone wants a TV, you go find it and bring it out. You don't have to convince someone to buy the TV, you don't have to argue over the price of the TV and your salary doesn't depend on you selling the TV. There are not a million different personalities that you have to deal with. Not the inattentive parent that lets their kids run screaming through the store. Not the jackass coworker that's trying to snake your commission. Not the guy that thinks he's entitled to a discount because the DVD player he wants isn't in stock. In the warehouse the only person you sincerely have to talk to is the truck driver and even then you only have to talk to them if something is missing or broken.

There are certainly downsides. For one, spending 40 hours a week tossing around boxes can feel a little Sisyphean. Also, there's not much money to be made in unskilled labor. Still, if I had to get a retail job I'd choose the warehouse over the sales floor every time. I don't mind helping people; I just don't want to have to deal with them.

I worked at Circuit City for three years before things fell apart. The company starting showing the chinks in their armor when they stopped paying commissions. This didn't affect me but plenty of people in the front of the house were upset. Inevitably people started getting laid off. Luckily I wasn't one of those people but around this time the managers started paying more attention to the warehouse. This was a problem not because we were doing anything illegal but because there wasn't much for us to do. If they found out that we were napping in the rafters or watching DVDs on the repaired TV's they would probably start cutting hours. Our fears were absolutely right.

One day one of the new managers came walking through a near empty warehouse. I don't think she was looking for anything or anyone but she found me; in a corner of the warehouse under a big screen TV fortress that I had built for myself reading a book. She asked me what I was doing and I told her truthfully that I was reading. I think she would have been less upset if it hadn't appeared to be hiding. She went to the store manager and reported me and the next day I was fired. I probably could have saved myself from firing if I had been more lovable and less curmudgeonly during those last few months when they were looking for ways to save money.

To be honest I thought I was bulletproof. I thought that I could do whatever I wanted as long as I got my work done. My coworkers were surprised when they heard the news. I was the most knowledgeable person there; I was well liked by everyone, and was always helpful. But I didn't have any work to do and I thought that gave me license to use my work hours as my own personal time. If I'm being totally honest with myself I still kind of feel that way. (I'm actually writing this book on company time at my current job.) The truth is, it didn't matter how I felt. After being fired I was escorted out of the building by the same coworker I had trained a month before.

Getting fired from a real job (as opposed to an internship) for the first time is a surreal experience. I remember sitting across from my boss wondering if this was all just an elaborate prank. I just knew that at any moment someone was going to burst into the room and start pointing out the cameras. When I finally hear the word "terminated" I felt just as embarrassed as if it had been a prank without the relief of knowing that I still had a job. My only consolation was that I hadn't been fired for nefarious reasons. I didn't attack anyone, I didn't steal anything, I didn't send dick-pics to my coworkers. I got fired for being apathetic and indifferent towards my work duties.

The first half of my walk home a storm cloud hung over my head until I realized something: I hated working there. I never had to go back to that place again. I had been working two jobs for the past three years. For the first time in months I finally had the afternoon off. I went home and got some sleep.

I later found out that shortly after I was fired Bob was laid off. They hired him back a few months later at a fraction of what he was originally getting paid. Six months after that Circuit City went bankrupt and I'd be lying if I said it didn't add a little spring to my step when I thought about my old boss having to look for a new job.

While I was working at Circuit City I was also working for Williams-Sonoma. Once again I worked in the warehouse. My co-workers were mostly older women who loved cooking. Unfortunately that wasn't the clientele. The customers were mostly upper-class novices that thought that if they spent more money their food would taste better. My boss was Anahita. She was truly one of my favorite bosses.

Everyone who worked there got along with everyone else and we all loved Anahita. Even when the restaurant above us developed a rat problem that eventually seeped into our store I was still happy to brave the warehouse to empty out the traps while she waited outside. The only person that didn't respect our close-knit family atmosphere was out district manager. She didn't care about our salespeople's dedication to epicurean teachings. What she cared about was sales and apparently we weren't doing much of it.

Before moving on I need to tell you a little more about our district manager. She was the type of person that was nonstop perky but that's not the worse part. What made her truly unbearable was that she used her sunshiny disposition to hide the fact that she had total disdain for everyone who worked underneath her. She was always smiling but she never had any good news.

One day out of the blue we were told that the store was moving. We would now be in the much bigger, newer mall across the street. We spent weeks packing up the store and relocating everything. One day we were moving to the new store and we were using her SUV to move some things that were too precious for the moving van. I and a few other people hopped in her ride and once she turned the ignition I heard the voice of Cee-Lo Green through the speakers. I've been a fan of Cee-Lo since Goodie Mob's first album *Soul Food.* His verse on "Live from the O.M.N.I." changed my life. I even bought his first solo albums when no one else would. When I heard that he had hooked up with Danger Mouse I was ecstatic. Finally, Cee-Lo would get the respect that he deserved. But when I heard "Crazy" pumping through the speakers of my district managers' soccer mom SUV I had such a visceral reaction that I haven't listened to Cee-Lo Green since. Also, within 3 months time she would eventually fire everyone riding in her SUV on that day.

I tried my best to get the store in shape after the move but there were quite a few things working against me. Anahita was forced to hire a bunch of high school students that weren't as industrious as I was hoping they would be. They couldn't organize anything the way I needed them to and because they were teenagers they had minimal work schedules. To make matters worse Thanksgiving was approaching and the warehouse was still disorganized and cluttered because of the move. I was also working two jobs at the time. (After I was fired from Circuit City I got a job at Office Depot. More on that later.) The final straw was when I went on vacation. I knew that it was a bad idea to leave while the store was in shambles but I was going out of the county and there was no way for me to postpone my trip. Besides I had been planning this vacation for months and my time off had already been approved. On my last day before my vacation Anahita suspended me and told me we would talk when I got back. When I got back Anahita herself had been suspended and I was fired. Within a month everyone that had helped move the store had been replaced.

After being fired for a second time I thought a lot about what I wanted to do. My first thought was to find another job. I realized fairly quickly that I didn't want another "job". I needed to find a career. The tough part was realizing that I had been searching for a career for years but nothing I had ever tried had panned out. I thought I was going to be a writer, a recording engineer, a rapper, etc. I had failed at all of them. That I knew. The hardest part was figuring out why. Was it because I hadn't worked hard enough or was it because I just wasn't talented? The answer was going to be pretty painful no matter what my response was. At what point are you supposed to stop chasing your dream? I know, I know; you're never supposed to stop chasing your dream but have you ever met someone that has NEVER stopped chasing their dream. It's pretty pathetic. How are you supposed to decide if the effort isn't worth it anymore?

I decided I needed to go back to school. I didn't know much but I knew that if I was to go back this time I needed to know why I was going. I literally and figuratively couldn't afford to waste any time. Because I didn't know what else to do I paid $50 to take an online placement test to give me some guidance.

It stated that I enjoyed "creative activities". Knowing that creative activities didn't pay any money I kept reading. It said, "When I are working effectively, I tend to be reflective and systematic. To be most effective, I respond best to people who are reflective and creative. When people don't deal with me the way my needs suggest, I am likely to become self-critical and hesitant." I didn't know what any of this meant so I skipped down to see what jobs it suggested. In all there were about 15 different career choices but I decided to pick from the top three. The first groups of jobs were the Knowledge Specialists: Public school counselors, Psychologist, Career counselors, etc. The next was Legal. The third was Artistic.

Seeing as my main goal was to make money I immediately dropped the third choice. Morally I didn't think I could stomach being a lawyer so that Fall I enrolled in Psychology courses. I had no idea what I was doing but already I was more focused than I was last time around.

While I was figuring all of this out I still had a job at Office Depot. There was no real warehouse in Office Depot so I worked on the sales floor. This was fine with me because as long as I didn't have to work in electronics or office furniture I didn't have to actually sell anything. No one needed to be tricked into buying printer paper.

The manager that hired me hired me at the lowest possible wage of six dollars an hour. I'm fairly confident that if he could have legally paid me less he would have. Within a few months he was unceremoniously fired. Until the day I left we got a new store manager every few months.

I used to work 8 hours at Williams-Sonoma, and then walk across the street to start my 5-hour shift at Office Depot. After I was fired from Williams-Sonoma Office Depot became my primary job. O D holds a special place in my heart because it was my last hourly job where I had to punch in and out every day. This was also the first time in five years I hadn't worked two jobs. But I was also a full time student so my workload didn't decrease in any significant way.

I worked at Office Depot long enough to have done every job except manage. I even worked the overnight shift when the store remodeled. During my time there I met a coworker that would eventually become my best friend and eventually introduce me to my wife. More importantly I also met Jermaine Jackson, KRS-One, & Larenz Tate.

My last position before I left was as the Copy and Print Lead. This wasn't an official title. It basically meant that while I wasn't being paid as a manager I could pretty much do all the managerial stuff. My real manager was a woman named Amira. All of her regular customers loved her although most of them didn't know her name. They simply referred to her as "the Indian girl." This always bothered me because 1) she was Ethiopian and 2) she was in her 40s and therefore not a "girl". She never called anyone out on any of this though.

The reason people loved her was because she had a demeanor that was both manic and calming. She had a high-pitched voice that always seemed to be yelling but was never threatening; like a Muppet that you took seriously. Sometimes I wondered if this was all just an act. It was like she took the direction of George Costanza to heart: if you always look annoyed people will think that you're busy.

Amira was the face of the copy center while the rest of us that worked there were the backbone. She took all the orders and made the customer feel like their jobs would be done to perfection and in a reasonable amount of time. But it was up to me to do most of the work. I never got mad at her for this though because when something went wrong she could always smooth it over. She knew that it was nearly impossible for anyone to be upset with her and she took full advantage of it.

Working in the Copy Center was at times harder than working on the floor. If you sell a printer that doesn't work the customer doesn't blame you personally for creating a faulty piece of machinery. The same can't be said for botching a customer's 300-page thesis paper on The Effects of Tecate Music on South American Mice. The amount of accountability created a separation between the copy center and everyone else. We could do any of their jobs but none of them could do ours. This was the first time in my work history where this was true. Before then the only thing any of my jobs required of me was that I had a warm body and that I was physically able to lift things. True, what I was doing wasn't brain surgery but it involved more than moving a box from location A to location B. There were plenty of nights that I went to sleep with nightmares of a never-ending paper jam.

In all the jobs I had in my adult life customers and coworkers alike had always told me that I was too smart for the job that I had. I'm sure they meant it as a complement but I always took it as a judgment that I wasn't living up to my full potential. They were basically telling me that I was wasting my life.

I worked for Office Depot for five years and I'm proud to say I wasn't fired. I gave a two-week notice and unceremoniously walked out the front door on my last day. It felt good not having to be escorted out of the premises. It felt even better to know that I was leaving my job to because I had a better one lined up.

...

Going back to school was one of the hardest decisions I've ever had to make. To me going back to school was accepting that I failed. I wanted to be an artist but my art didn't seem to be good enough for anyone but me. How long do you have to lose before you call it quits? I had given up on school when I was 10. Now here I was 20 years later crawling back to it. The whole experience was humbling.

My first year back I took school very seriously. I recorded every class and then transcribed the notes only my laptop. Because of this I made the Dean's list my first semester back. Of course I was taking pretty basic courses but an A is an A. During my second semester I received a letter from an honor society asking me if I would be interested in joining. It was a program that helped underserved students prepare for PhD programs. I knew that in the field of psychology I needed more than a bachelor's degree but I wasn't sure I wanted to get a PhD. In the end I decided that it was worth it and accepted the invitation. I interviewed to become a part of the program and was accepted. By the summer I quit Office Depot to become a research assistant for California State University, Northridge.

Being a research assistant was actually pretty great. Essentially I was a student that was paid to do research and go to conferences. I didn't get paid enough to buy food but it paid for my classes so in the grand scheme of things I was breaking even. It was also a program that taught us how to write curriculum vita's, personal statements, and what people want to see on college applications. This particular job was without a doubt the most important one I ever had.

Unfortunately, once I graduated I was no longer eligible. In the back of my mind I always knew this but it didn't hit me until about a week before I graduated that I was going to be unemployed when I started grad school in the fall.

I spent the entire summer months looking for a job. That three months was the longest I had ever been unemployed since I was 16. It was also the most relaxing/stressful summer I've ever had. A few weeks before school started I got a job with a wine distributer. It was a small enough company to where you could see the president walking through the halls but big enough to where the top-level employees were millionaires.

I got the job because one of those millionaires was starting a new division in the company and needed new faces to test it out on. My official title was "Product Handler". My job was to show up at stores between 6 and 7 am and help "handle" our product. I couldn't take the product off the truck because that was the truck drivers' job and they were union. I couldn't put the product on the shelf because due to a few laws that were created after prohibition ended in 1933 it's illegal for a non-employee to place alcohol on the shelf. I did everything in between.

The truck driver would unload the product and then I would place the product on the floor in front of where it went on the shelf. We did this as a courtesy to the stores so that they would let us display our product more prominently. Some stores appreciated our help while others wanted us to stay out. It only took a few weeks to learn which stores where which.

While it was considered a full time job where I got paid full time hours I typically started work at 6AM and was finished by 10AM. The only time I worked a full 8-hour shift was on the days when I had to help build a new store. Whenever a liquor store opened up a new location my bosses would volunteer us to help build and stock their shelves. Even though this was usually hard work these were usually my favorite days. When the day was over there was physical evidence that I actually accomplished something.

The Product Handler was the lowest person on the totem pole. Most of the people only had the job a few months before they were promoted to Sales Representative. I was a Product Handler for 2 years. This was partly because it was the perfect stress-free job to have while I was in grad school. But it was also because I didn't want the responsibility of being a Sales Representative.

As a Product Handler I was in charge of moving product from A to B. I wasn't expected to sell anything and I hardly ever saw my boss. As a Sales Rep your boss is always keeping tabs on you to make sure you're moving the product and keeping a smile on the store managers' face.

As I got closer to graduation I started applying for new jobs. This included jobs with my current employers' home office and research jobs where I could actually use my degree. I applied for a job with the home office because I actually did like the company. The people at the top weren't geniuses. They didn't have business school degrees. I'm pretty sure most of them probably didn't even go to college. I remember one meeting where we celebrating the fact that one of the hire-ups had finally received her bachelor's degree.

They were just men and women that put in their time, kissed some ass and sold a lot of booze. Now I wasn't planning on kissing a bunch of ass or selling a bunch of booze but I was happy to work at a place where everyone at the top started out as a Sales Rep. They weren't hired just because their father was the presidents' golf buddy.

I never got a research job and I never got hired in the home office but I did get offered a Sales Rep position. I figured if I accepted the Sales Rep job I'd have a better chance of getting a job in the home office. The job was exactly what I expected. The Product Handler job was solitary while the Sales Reps were assigned to teams. My team covered all of the San Fernando Valley. I would come later to realize that the San Fernando Valley was like the Island of Misfit Toys. They sold their fair share of booze but kissed significantly less ass and because of that they were exiled to uncooperative stores with less foot traffic. My San Fernando Valley Team had accepted their fate but that didn't stop them from complaining about it.

I never stopped looking for a new job. I thought that every Friday would be my last. I felt that way for 52 consecutive Fridays. After countless interviews with other agencies and multiple rejections I finally got a research position not because of my impressive resume but because I knew a person that knew a person.

...

Years ago when my teacher asked me what I wanted to do with my life I could have said "Be kind" or "Do something memorable" but of course that wasn't what she meant. She wanted to know how I was going to make money. What job did I want to have? And the truth was and still is that there is no job that I want to have. Sure, if someone asks me what I do I'll realize that they are asking me what my job is and I'll answer accordingly. I'm not a jerk. But I don't want to be the type of person that is defined by how they get paid. I want to raise a family, travel the world and skateboard. To me a job, and yes even a career, is a thing I do to get money to facilitate those things and nothing more.

Chapter 13: Failing at Money

At 13 when I first started in the wood business my grandmother offered to put the money my grandfather paid me into a savings account. She offered this deal to all my cousins. I, like all my cousins, declined. My grandfather paid me about $20 a day. In the summer I worked for him 5 times a week. The rest of the year I worked on the weekends. That comes to about 140 days a year, which comes to $2,800 a year, tax-free. If I did the exact same thing every year until I was 16 with an annual compound interest rate of 1% I would have started out my adult life with $11,453.97 in the bank. I have no regrets because no 13 year old in history would have been willing to work as hard as I was for 3 years without seeing any benefit. Well, maybe my grandfather.

I bought video games, candy, and new clothes but the only thing I bought that truly drained my bank account was music. I can still remember the smell of the music store around the corner from my house. This was mostly because they also sold ethnic hair care products. To this day the smell of pink lotion and Shea butter always reminds me of early 90s R&B. Within my first year of working I filled 3 shoeboxes with neatly alphabetized audiocassettes.

What really did me in was the year 1994. In those 365 days hip hop could do no wrong: Nas *Illmatic*, Notorious B. I. G. *Ready to Die*, Outkast *Southerplayalisticadillacmuzik*, Warren G. *Regulate... G Funk Era*, Bone Thugs-N-Harmony, *Creepin' on ah Come Up*. And that's just the A-listers. There was also UGK *Super Tight*, Redman *Dare Iz a Darkside*, Big Mike *Somethin' Serious*, Spice 1 *AmeriKKKa's Nightmare*, Da Brat, *Funkdafied*, etc. There was a time in 1994 when you could go to the hip hop section blindfolded and pick out your new favorite album. For the next 10 years of my life this is basically how I bought music. In that time I bought roughly 5,000 CDs at a time when they cost about $20 each. If you're keeping score that's $100,000. I currently only own about 1,000 of the CDs I purchased as a 20 year old. That's $80,000 wasted on Limp Bizkit, 311, and Incubus records. I wish I could tell you that I got rid of most of my physical music collection because I saw the error in my ways. The truth is I was just tired of lugging them around every time I moved.

...

The first time I used a credit card it was actually a fairly noble affair: I was buying textbooks for my first semester in college. I walked out of the store stunned by how easy it was. Before then I had only paid cash or written checks. When you hand over cash or write a check it's gone forever. It will never come back to you in the same way. But when you hand over a credit card it comes back looking exactly the same as if nothing had changed. And it only took a few seconds. You didn't have to count money and pretend that you knew how much change you were suppose to get back. You didn't have to write a check and hear everyone in line behind you release a collective sigh. One swipe and everything you requested was now yours. It's magical.

But I'm getting ahead of myself. Let's back up to the day I first starting getting mail. After I turned 17 corporations no longer had to ask for my parents' permission to talk to me. My dad was no longer the only Mr. Tillman in the household.

Corporations were now able to ask me if I wanted magazines. They could ask if I wanted CDs and cassettes. And most importantly they could ask me if I wanted $500 in the form of a credit card. How could I say no? Of course I didn't tell my parents about any of these offers. I was a grownup now. A grownup that still relied on his parents to house and feed me but a grownup nonetheless.

In my 20s I crucified myself with credit card debt the way most people do: by using it as a paycheck extension instead of using it as a tool to build credit. For instance, if I didn't have enough money to pay my car note I would use a credit card. This saved me for a few weeks until I had to pay the credit card bill. Most of the time I didn't have enough money to pay the card off so I made the minimum payment. The minimum payment would save me until next month when I had to pay the credit card bill that now has an interest fee tacked on. When it was time to pay the car note I still didn't have enough money so again I would use the credit card. This cycle repeated until the credit card was maxed out and now not only do I need to pay off the maxed out credit card but I also still needed to pay my car note. In just a few short months I had tripled my debt. The only thing left for me to do was suck the Devil's dick and get another credit card. Before I knew it my car was getting repossessed and my credit score was in the low 300s.

The best way to prevent this is to have a budget to make sure you can afford all the things you have. The problem with that is that if you're only making minimum wage you can't afford anything. Six dollars an hour is fine if you're 16 and living with your parents but not if you're on your own eating soup out of a can every night. Who can blame someone for wanting more out of his or her life than that? Sure you can survive but there has to be more to life than just making it through to the other side.

Although my immediate fanatical troubles were rooted in credit card spending the long-term damage was done by my student loans. Before I applied for financial aid my mom told me that I would also get extra money for living expenses. I took this to mean that I was to take all the money that I could. I didn't understand that I was only supposed to take what I needed. Just because the government offered me $10,000 didn't mean I had to take $10,000. Also, I didn't know the difference between a loan and a grant. I still barely understand the difference between a subsidized and an unsubsidized loan. And I wish to lower cased god that I had known of the relentlessness of a private loan.

This damage could have been mitigated had I not attended and dropped out of so many different schools.

How I Racked up College Loan Debt in 10 Short Years				
Years	Public or Private	College or University	Drop out or Graduate	Degree
2	Public	College	Graduate	Useless
2	Public	University	Drop out	None
1	Private	College	Drop out	None
3	Public	University	Graduate	Useful
2	Public	University	Graduate	Useful

I racked up a decade of school loans with not much to show for it. I should have a medical degree with the amount of time and money I put in. While I was in school my loans never crossed my mind. Because I dropped out I knew I wasn't getting a job that would be able to pay what I needed but I figured everything would work itself out. Of course it didn't and before long I was getting letters in the mail detailing my impending doom. Lucky for me I was moving around so much that they would never find me. Right? Of course they found me and before I knew it I was getting *phone calls* detailing my impending doom. So I did the logical thing: I started dodging calls. This was pretty easy to do because they only had my home phone. This went on for 5 years.

When I decided to go back to school I played things a little smarter. I studied up and applied for as many grants and scholarships as I could find. I didn't get enough to pay my full tuition so I still had to get loans but I only took as much as I though I needed. Also, now that I was back in school the loan offices stopped calling. The grace period had been extended until I graduated. The loans would still collect interest however the grace period didn't apply to the private loan. Fucking private loans.

After my first year I got a job on campus that didn't interrupt my studies. In my last year of grad school I saved up enough money to pay everything out of pocket. After I graduated I vowed never to get another student loan again. I should be finished paying off my current loans sometime between now and when my grandchild is born.

...

In America our core belief is that if a person is rich it is because they worked hard for it and they did it on their own. Clearly that's not true in all cases but it does ring true more often than not. Unfortunately the flipside of that coin is that if you're poor it's your own fault. Why didn't you just work harder? This is why people buy houses they may not be able to afford, buy brand name clothes that will be out of fashion is months, and buy smart phones that are less and less impressive every year. Having money means you're independent. You worked hard and you were rewarded. No one wants to be in the other category: The people that weren't smart enough to figure out the code. The people that didn't work hard enough and are now being punished for their shiftlessness. The ones that just couldn't get it together.

If a person becomes rich we feel it must mean that they are good at what they do. At the very least we feel that they were lucky. In the case of lottery winners we mean this literally. If that same person goes broke then they must be stupid. We think about all the things we would have done differently if we were in their position. In social psychology this is called the "fundamental attribution error" and the "actor-observer bias".

The fundamental attribution error is the tendency for one to place more emphasis on internal characteristics to explain someone else's behavior rather than considering the external factors. The opposite of this is called the actor-observer bias. It's when one places more emphasis on internal characteristics to explain their own behavior rather than considering the internal factors. In short if *you* cut *me* off in traffic it's because you're an idiot that doesn't know how to drive. If *I* cut *you* off in traffic it's because I have a lot of things on my mind.

In reality most Americans don't know much about basic economics. We don't understand the stock market or interest rates. Beyond a 401K we don't know how to save for retirement. So what would we have done differently? The reality is that a person made a mistake that got out of hand. If people that were constantly trying to take all of my money surrounded me I would probably be bankrupt too. But no one is trying to rob a guy that makes 30K a year. That's like going to the Sistine Chapel to look at the floor tiles. You should probably set your goals a little higher.

Chapter 14: Failing at Christianity

I was nine years old the first time I stepped inside a church. Until then, Sunday was just the second day of the weekend. Although my parents grew up in the church they stopped attending at some point in their adulthood. That all ended when we moved back to Texas. Well, the first few years my parents still refused to go but eventually they came back around.

I never had any strong feelings about having to go to church, it just felt like another entry onto an ever expanding list of things grownups where making me do. I wouldn't call going to church a burden but it was defiantly a chore. I didn't like the crowds, or the songs (actually the songs weren't that bad. It was me having to sing along to them that I hated) and the speech at the end was hardly worth staying awake for.

For about 5 years my siblings and me went to church with our grandmothers. My maternal grandmothers' church was buttoned down. There was not a lot of screaming and shouting that one usually thinks of when one thinks of southern Black churches. The pastor revved things up a bit for the last 10 minutes of his sermon but for the most part it was a pretty somber occasion. My paternal grandmother's church was defiantly more raucous. There was a live band, people catching the "holy ghost" and their broadcast was even on the radio. Even with these striking differences I still had no preference for either. Aside from when my cousin Stephen and I made fun of the choir it was all just white noise. None of it seemed like it meant anything.

Around the time I turned 13 my parents remembered their Christian values and decided to go to church again. They found a storefront church on the other side of town and one Sunday they drove us there without warning. By now I was used to the idea of going to church and didn't see it as a chore. Now it felt more like a routine. Like turning on the TV when you get home, it just felt like something to make your room/life feel less empty.

The storefront church had fewer people and a much different demographic than I was used to. Practically everyone who attended my grandmother's churches had been a member their whole lives. They met their spouses, had children and raised their children all at the same church. In other words, the people that went to church at my grandmother's churches were "church people". Service at the storefront church felt a little like an AA meeting. This church was where people go after they hit bottom. This was where poor families got free breakfast and where former prostitutes and/or drug addicts got saved. I can only imagine what my parents had to go through to end up there.

My father was in charge of recording the church service every Sunday. He took care of the sound check and made sure the equipment worked correctly. It was my job to turn over the cassette tape at the 45-minute mark. I also helped label and passed them out at the end of the service. It was the only thing that kept me awake.

One thing that was the same at every church I attended was the inherent separatism. Men were constantly being separated from the women. In every church I attended there were Deacons and Ladies (or in more progressive churches "Deaconesses"). As far as I could tell the Deacons were there to hang around the pastor, count the money and give the pastor advice. A deacon had to be ordained although I'm pretty sure the only requirement was that you had to at least have a 40-year-old prostate. I don't recall ever seeing a Lady/Deaconess being ordained. Maybe you didn't need to be ordained to sit around the pastors' wife, teach the children Sunday school and prepare church dinners. Maybe their ordination was when they started menstruation.

I personally disliked the adults being separated from the children. The Sunday school lessons for children never changed. Every lesson was about David and Goliath, Noah and the Ark or Jesus and his Miracles. I imagined there had to be more to our religion than a bunch of silly stories but judging from what I learned in Sunday school that was all there was.

The worst part was when the teacher tried to relate these stories to our everyday struggles at school. "When someone pressures you to do something you know is wrong trust in God like David, Noah, and Jesus" because it all worked out for those guys. Then we would color a picture and wait for the adults to call us to join the congregation. The older I got the more unbearable this became. After a few years I asked to sit with the adults during Sunday school. Since my father was the teacher this was a pretty easy thing to get done. I couldn't wait to sit with the adults and get the real scoop on what all this was about. I was bummed to find out that everything I learned in Sunday school was pretty much it. The stories were a little more obscure but all in all it was the same message: trust god and don't ask too many questions.

After a few years at the storefront church my parents felt that they had gained all they could and moved on to a bigger church. My parents insisted that they moved to this church for our sake. The high school I was attending was predominantly white and the church we were attending had no children my age so they felt our new church would be a better fit. And I have to say they made a pretty good call. My grandmothers' churches were literally 100 years old. This new church was 30, tops. There were kids there my age and adults my parents' age that hadn't been to prison or sucked dick for money. I felt like Goldilocks after she ate the baby bears porridge. It was just right. To this day when I think of my home church this is where I hang my hat. I'm still friends or at least acquaintances with most of the people I met here. I spent the remainder of my teenage years there.

This did not mean that I enjoyed it there. By this time church was not a chore or a routine. By now it felt kind of dangerous. I remember Sundays where I would look around the congregation amazed and a little sad that we were still doing all of this. We all came to the same place week after week to hear the same stories that we had heard since we were children. By now we've heard the whole story at least a dozen times. Why are we still here?

I had friends that were clearly gay but they still came to this building every week to be told that there were going to Hell. There were women who weren't ready to completely close the door on their hedonistic pasts but they still came every week to sing in the choir. There were grown men that snuck out of service so they could catch the tail end of the football game. I couldn't understand why all these people were still there. Moreover, I couldn't understand why people were still getting saved. How is it possible to grow up in America and not know who Jesus is? How is it that you're 40 years old and Jesus dying on the cross for your sins in new information? To make matters worse, the last 15 minutes of every sermon at that church ended the exact same way. Literally. Word for word. Every. Sunday.

By the time I went away to college I was elated. I would never have to go to church again if I didn't want to. The thing was I kind of wanted to. As frustrated as I was, in my heart I understood why all those people still went to church; they felt obligated. It wasn't just a building; it was a part of your culture.

It's hard to turn your back on the culture that made you feel like you belonged and gave you a little hope when you needed it. The same culture that saved my parents. Not just in the religious sense. Without the church asking them to turn their life around I can't imagine who they would have become.

When I went away to college I did go to church for a few weeks. One Sunday I was broke and I knew that if I went to church I would use up the precious gas I needed to go to work the next day. I decided I would step out on faith and prayed that God would work a miracle. The next day on my way to work I ran out of gas. I flagged down a police officer that gave me a ride in the back of his squad car (I assume this was protocol) to a gas station where I spent my last $3 on gas. Maybe God sent the cop my way to help. Fair enough. But it still didn't help that I had no money and no gas to get back home.

My walk with God changed a little after this. I began to ask, "What if the Christian God is wrong?" "What if I'm the baddie for not worshipping Allah or Ganesh or the extremely misunderstood Dark Lord Satan?" I read The Koran, The Tao Te Ching, I read modern and ancient philosophers and for a while I thought I had it figured out. I spent years getting further and further away from what I had grown up with until one day it finally happened. I was on a beach in Cancun Mexico, I was having a conversation with someone about religion and for the first time I referred to myself as an atheist. I was 29. It had been 10 years since I voluntarily stepped inside a church and this was the first time I felt relieved by that fact. For 10 years I struggled to find out what God was trying to tell me only to realize that it wasn't trying to tell me anything.

…

I don't know if you've ever taken a Pure Tone Audiometry hearing test before but it goes something like this: A doctor or nurse puts headphones on you and plays tones at different frequencies and in alternating ears. When you hear a sound you signify it by pushing a button with your left or right hand to signify which ear you heard the sound.

I was once given this test as part of a physical before I was hired for a job. The woman administering the test must have had other things to do because she left the room immediately after she put the headphones on my head. She did not tell me how long this test would last or if there would be any signal when it was over. I sat there pushing buttons for about five minutes before the noises stopped. Or at least I think they did. I listened intently for the next few minutes waiting for the next sound. It was an excruciating experience because if I didn't pass this physical I wouldn't get the job and I wouldn't be able to buy ramen noodles in Korea Town. I would have been relegated to instant ramen noodles from in the supermarket. I listened intently for what felt like hours until I realize "Hey, I think the test is over." I relaxed my ears and breathed a sigh of relief. I'm telling you this story because this was the exact felling I felt when I realized that there is no god. There is no tiny voice trying to get your attention. You can relax.

For me the hardest part of admitting to myself that I was an atheist was turning my back on my upbringing. It's hard to separate the nostalgia I feel towards the rituals of my childhood and my inability to believe in any of that stuff anymore. This is something that people that grew up without religion never have to deal with and I kind of envy them for it. On the other hand I'm probably a better atheist because I came to the realization on my own instead of having it spoon fed to me when I was a baby.

If you step off of the curb and twist your ankle there are many ways to perceive that:

"God is trying to punish me."

"The universe is trying to teach me a lesson."

"I'm an idiot that doesn't know how to walk."

No matter your perception, your reality is that you twisted your ankle. Belief in God may be able to help you cope but it'll never change your reality.

Religion eliminates a lot of the existential guesswork. If something terrible happens, or things don't go your way you don't have to rack your brain trying to figure out why it happened. You can just say it was God's will. I have no real qualms with religion because without it life seems pretty bleak. Who do you blame when someone you love dies unexpectedly? What do you do when you have to take a test that you're not completely ready for? What are you supposed to do with the mystery of death? You mean to tell me that one day I just won't exist anymore? I'll admit that believing in Heaven and Hell is much more comforting but for me the fear is what makes life so important.

I don't believe that there is one big plan but a series of small ones that humans have made up as we go along. I might be completely wrong but like I've already said, I don't think it matters. Belief in God won't keep your husband from leaving you, it won't prevent your daughter from being born with a rare skin disease and it won't keep you from being laid off at the plant but it can help you cope with that stuff. That's the reason I don't hate religion. It has its purpose. I might not need it but I understand that some people do.

What I don't understand is angry atheist. What's to be upset about: you get to sleep in late on Sundays, there's no fasting, or unnecessary guilt, no food restrictions, no trips to holy lands, no interrupting your day to get out your prayer mat, etc. The only downside to atheism is constantly feeling like the sober person at a party. You have to watch all the people you know and love do and say the most ridiculous things and there's nothing you can do because you can't argue with a drunken person. You might think that sounds smug and condescending and you would be absolutely right. Being smug and condescending is just one of the many perks of being an atheist.

Chapter 15: Failing at Sports

I don't like sports. It's not because I think they're barbaric, or because they reward violence, or anything like that. In all honesty I wish I liked sports. They bring people together. Honestly, would millions of Americans learn how to properly spell Dwyane Wade if he couldn't put a ball in a hoop? There is no other topic in America that most people know/care about that is also fairly inoffensive. Hell, half the fun of talking about sports is getting into arguments.

I hate the look people get on their face when I tell them I don't watch sports. It's a look of bewilderment and sadness that they can't share with me one of the few things that matter in the world. Like a Jehovah's Witness after you've told them you're not interested.

I also feel that major league sports are the only true meritocracy in America. If you're a poor child of a sharecropper who grew up in the backwoods of Mississippi who's also good at math, no one from MIT is going to come to your house to eat with your family and then offer you a million dollar contract. In sports it doesn't matter what ethnicity you are, your socioeconomic circumstances, or how many people you rape, if you can properly fondle a ball everyone around you will bond together to make sure you live a successful lifestyle for a few years (unless you're a girl).

No, the reason why I don't like sports is because I can't make myself care enough. To be fair this feeling actually extends to all games. I lost interest in board games when I was 5, video games when I was 13, and team building exercises the moment I discovered they existed. I can appreciate someone's skill and hard work but I just don't care about the outcome. I can't even comprehend how someone roots for a team that doesn't include a close family member. But the arbitrary idea of picking a favorite team really frustrates me.

How to Choose A Major League Sports Team

As a kid I had a baseball/football/basketball card

collection because that's what other boys my age had. When I

went to the mall I would buy packs of cards with whatever

money I had saved up. I would buy magazines that told me

which cards were the most valuable. I bought plastic pouches to make sure none of my cards ever got bent and a binder to keep all of them safe. The only problem was that I didn't watch any of the games so I had no idea who any of the players were. My favorite card was a 1989 Pepper Johnson from when he played with the New York Giants right after they won the Super Bowl. I didn't actually know who Pepper Johnson was but I liked the card because his name was "Pepper". I mean who names their child 'Pepper'? (I only learned while writing this book that his real name is Thomas.) I'm almost certain I gave away some great cards when I traded with my friends. For me it was all about the photograph. I had no idea what any of their stats meant. It took me a few years to find out that I didn't know what I was doing and I eventually gave up. I kept my cards for a while but eventually gave them away to my foster brothers before I moved out. They probably sold them for drugs. Not hard drugs, probably just weed.

In junior high I learned that the best way for me to survive gym class was to be as invisible as possible. When we played flag football I played defense and never asked for the ball. This was because no matter the outcome of the play if I showed any type of skill it would always turn out bad for me. If I made a bad play someone on my team would yelled at me and possibly punch me in the chest. If I made a good play the other team would yell at me and *defiantly* punch me in the chest. Why, you ask? Because I was the unpopular kid who wasn't on the football team and I wasn't supposed to make good plays. They wanted to make sure that I thought twice about embarrassing them again. Sometimes I obliged. Sometimes I didn't. I was like Andy Dufresne in The Shawshank Redemption. Only instead of being raped I was being roughed up a little. Besides than that: exactly the same.

In gym class when we played baseball I was the pitcher but not because I was any good. Actually it was the exact opposite. My only job was to lob softballs over the plate. Because everything I threw was meant for maximum contact I didn't have to run or catch. If my team wanted to win this game it was up to them. It didn't matter to me at all. I was just waiting for the bell to ring so that this torture could be over.

There were a few times I played games willingly outside of class. During lunch breaks we would usually play Throw up Tackle although in some neighborhoods it is also known as "Smear the Queer". If you're not familiar with the game it's a version of street football where it's you verses everyone on the field. We would take anything that could be comfortably caught, throw it up in the air, and tackled whoever dared catch it. Ideally this is usually played with an actual football or if you're in a pinch a tennis ball but more often than not we played with a crushed soda can.

As long as it was a game amongst my friends (i.e. not the guys on the football team) I usually joined in. We would usually play in the open field behind the school. On the far end of the field was a creek that we used as the out of bounds marker. It was narrow enough to jump across but was about 8 feet deep. It was mostly dry but there were still a few inches of water running through it.

One day after school I was having a particularly good game. (To be honest the only skill you need to be good at Throw up Tackle is the ability to run away from large groups of people. I was a natural.) One strategy that was typically used was to run along the creek so that no one tackled you. If you fell in your pursuer would fall in after you so as long as you didn't lose your balance no one would touch you. It was genius. Ok, maybe I was the only one that utilized this strategy but I thought it was pretty smart. But one day I flew too close to the sun.

My friend Brandon Thompson knocked me into the creek while he looked over me laughing. Luckily I landed on a ledge that was only 5 feet down so I spared myself the wet clothes. I landed on my face and the lenses of my glasses left a crescent shaped cut on my face. I still sport a teardrop scar on the outside of my left eye. To this day this remains my only sports related injury.

By the time I got to High school I came to the realization that I didn't actually like sports and there was no point in trying to pretend. Somehow this newfound knowledge didn't stop me from playing sports. This was because there was very little else to do at my high school. Literally every guy I went to school with was on the soccer or basketball team. The school was so small that they couldn't afford to turn anyone away so there was little in the way of tryouts. This was good because I was pretty bad at soccer. I could never get used to the idea of not using my hands. To this day I still can't properly kick a soccer ball more than 5 feet.

Our soccer team was pretty good with no thanks to me. We always made it to the finals but in my four years at the school we ever won. Most of my memories of playing soccer had to do with me standing on the field hoping the ball never came my way. After my freshman and sophomore years I decided I had had enough and I sat my junior year out. But I was talked into playing again my senior year. Not because the team needed me but because it was my senior year. This might be my last chance to play soccer; a sport I was no good at and didn't like. How could I say no?

I remember my first practice after I came back. It was in the pouring rain and I had grown an afro over the summer. If you've ever stood shivering in the middle of a soccer field with an afro full of rainwater then you'll know why I was having second thoughts about rejoining the team. Somehow I stuck with it, we went to the finals, got second place and a few weeks later basketball season started.

I'm not much better at basketball than I am at soccer. The only real difference is that I kind of enjoy playing basketball. Or at least I like playing it more than soccer. I was never good enough for varsity, which was always embarrassing when underclassmen received the privilege.

For most of my tenure I was the only Black kid in the league. This intimidated most of the other teams until they saw me play. I think I broke a few racial stereotypes in those years. My biggest problem was that I had zero confidence in my skills. I didn't trust myself to dribble the ball down court without it bouncing off my food into the stands. If anyone passed the ball to me I passed it back like we were playing an unsolicited game of Hot Potato.

Aside from confidence another thing I didn't have was a decent pair of basketball shoes. There were games where my shoes were so warn down that had I found the gumption to dribble down the court I wouldn't have been able to stop before I slid out of bounds. There were games where I slid around the court like a human blooper real.

In my senior year of high school my basketball team was invited to participate in a tournament in Tennessee. Only the Varsity team was invited but because I was a senior I got to tag along. Even though we won the regional championship, once we got to the tournament we immediately realized that we were out of our league. I only remember playing in one game. We were losing so bad that it didn't really matter anymore.

I completely forgot that I was in rural Tennessee until the other team gently reminded me. I was elbowed, shoved and kicked from the moment I stepped on the court. Somehow the referee didn't see any of it. It took a while for my coach to realize what was happening but once he did he pulled me out. I honestly think that might have been the last time I played an organized basketball game in my life.

...

I'm fully aware that some of my dislike of sports has to do with my fear of failing. I, much like Michel Jordan, hate to lose more than I love to win. But it can't all be about my fear of failing. I've failed at a lot of things. In fact, I've written an entire book about it. I guess my biggest problem is the lack of nuance. You begin as a participant and you end as either a winner or a loser. There is no in between. A tie game is basically two teams simultaneously losing.

Two people will try to kill each other over political views because they have alternate interpretations of the world. Those same two people can watch a soccer match together (provided they don't know each other's political views beforehand) because there's no alternate interpretation of a soccer match: either you score or you don't, either you win or you lose. If there is any disagreement we just consult the rulebook. The same things that make sports so universally revered are the same things that I find off-putting. Someone else has already decided on the limits and if you live up to them you win, if you fall short you lose. That doesn't sit well with me. As the 2 time presidential election "winner" George W. Bush once said, "I'm the decider."

Chapter 16: Failing at Family

I like my family. They're nice people. I would even go so far as to say that I love them. Before I get too mushy I need to inform you that I know that this love is spawned from the fact that they we share DNA and not much else. If my mother were trapped under a bus I could not summon the strength to lift it off of her. If my brother were hanging off the side of a cliff I wouldn't be able to single handedly pull him to safety. If my father needed a heart transplant I would not rip my own out of my chest and hand it to him. Instead I visit them occasionally and on even more rare occasions send them money but anything more than that is unlikely. I have the same level of intimacy with my family as I do with my Facebook friends. I wish them a happy birthday when prompted, ignore their political views and remain skeptical that they actually "like" anything I do.

I never set out to distance myself from my family. Like the spreading of Pangea or a crush being ushered into the "friend zone" it was just something that happened organically. On the date of my birth if I had been asked if I wanted to be a part of a family I defiantly would have declined. Throughout my life the most important thing to me was to always have my own space to do what I wanted. It's hard to do that when you're surrounded by people that are quietly judging you. Sometimes their judgment is right and sometimes it is needed but that's beside the point. If I was going to fail I needed to fail on my own. Some people live for the support of their family. I don't think I ever trusted anyone enough for that. Specifically, I never trusted that anyone else actually knew what they were doing. Since I was seven it seemed like to me that we were all just making it up as we went along. I've yet to be proven wrong.

It's not just me that is distant from my family. All my siblings are also pretty distant from each other. The main difference between them and me is that I think they wanted a close-knit family and were disappointed when they never got it. I never cared either way. They fight amongst themselves and sometimes go years without speaking. So far I have a perfect record of not giving a fuck. It's not because I don't care about them. It's that, good or bad, I don't judge what they do. This is more than likely spawned from my aversion to being judged. This is why even when they don't talk to each other they all talk to me.

This flies directly in the face of my mothers' ideals. She, like my father, came from a large family. She loved the idea of having a house full of siblings. After seeing pictures of my mom any her four younger sisters I often wondered if she (or her father) ever imagined them starting a band. This would have made her Jackie Jackson (or Rebbie Jackson if we're being gender specific) but I doubt this was ever the plan. She more idolized the Kennedys and their Catholic inability to use contraception. To this day my parents still have an assortments of foster/adopted children roaming their house.

During my junior year of high school my parents asked me how I felt about them having foster children live with us. They assured me that this wouldn't mean that they loved us any less. They wanted to know how I felt about someone else calling them "mom" and "dad". I barely understood the question. I couldn't tell if they were asking out of common courtesy or if they really were asking for my permission. On the one hand it would have been pretty weird had they started unloading kids into the house without telling anyone but I couldn't imagine that they would put everything on hold if I had said "no".

Either way I was a few years away from college and I sincerely did not care. The way I saw it they were grown people and if this was the decision they wanted to make I wasn't going to stand in their way. My older brothers were long gone so they were barley affected. The person I actually felt sorry for was my younger sister. She hadn't yet finished high school which meant that she had to endure this longer than any of us.

Months later when the kids started to move in, I didn't feel any different. The first girl they got was named Caroline. I never found out her whole story but it was obvious that she didn't want to be there. She wanted to be with her mother, which was impossible only because her mother was in jail. This, I would come to find out, was the story of most of the children that came through my parents doors. One day Caroline found out that one of her friends from foster care had been taken into a home nearby and she wanted to visit her. I somehow got roped into the visit.

My parents and the other foster parents, the Johnsons, set this up as sort of a play date. The Johnsons were a little corny but their waterfront home more than made up for their lack of cool. I left thinking that Caroline's friend Sylvia was living the life. Two days later Sylvia ran away. She wanted to be with her mom. I can't say this for a fact but judging by Sylvia's demeanor and speech pattern her mother did not live in a mini-mansion like the Johnson's. A few weeks later Caroline ran away herself. This was the first of Caroline's many attempts to break out.

Some of the kids appreciated what my parents did, others didn't. I can understand that. I can understand running away to live with your friends. I can understand running away

to ride the rails with your boy/girlfriend. I cannot understand

running away to live with your parents. I always felt like I was

lucky because I was born to parents that were nice, loving,

and nurturing. Had I been born to parents that abandoned me,

abused me, or couldn't provide for me better than I could

provide for myself I couldn't imagine wanting to run away to be

with them.

For the most part my interactions with the foster kids

were positive. They got on my nerves from time to time but it

was never unbearable. I only lost my temper once and that

one time permanently changed my thinking.

I was on break from school and came home to visit my

parents. I was driving my parents' minivan back from

somewhere with four of the kids with me. The three boys in the

backseats I knew. They were all teenagers and pretty well

behaved when they wanted to be. The one in the passenger

seat was named David. I didn't know him as well as I knew the

others. He was about eight and was the type of kid that would flip out in a grocery store if his mom told him he couldn't have ice cream. Sometimes he would kick and scream, other times he would sings obnoxious songs at the top of his lungs, but on this day he decided to go old school: he played a game I like to call "Why". It's very easy to play but no one ever wins. It's when a kid keeps asking "why" until you want to punch him in the face. Which is exactly what I did. Ok, I didn't *exactly* punch him in the face but I'm not any more proud of my decision.

David had just begun the lightning round of Why when I reached across without looking and hit him with the back of my hand. He immediately started wailing. In all honesty I meant to hit him in the chest but I miscalculated his height and my knuckle landed right on his nose. I didn't feel like I hit him that hard so I looked over to tell him to stop crying and was terrified when I saw that the entire front of his shirt was covered in blood. Everyone in the van including David immediately went into panic mode. Had I just punched my little brother in the face I probably could have dealt with my parents yelling at me for a few hours but this had the potential to ruin everything my parents had worked for. Not to mention I had just beat up an 8 year old.

The boys' imaginations sprang into action. The story they decided on was that David had been jumping around in the car and accidently smashed his face into the dashboard. I didn't take part in the negotiations but I didn't impede them either. As soon as I parked the van the boys rushed David to the bathroom where they washed his face and helped him rehearse his lines. I'll admit I was a little touched when I saw the amount of work they put in to try to protect me but I knew it wasn't right. So, I marched into my parents' room and told them everything that happened. Shortly after I started talking a shitless David walked into the room and tried to recite his speech but I told him stand down. My parents called the agency and told them what happened. As far as I know nothing ever came of it but I remember feeling pretty low. I apologized to David and told the boys I appreciated their efforts but I had to take responsibility for what I did.

There aren't a lot of things I'm ashamed of but if I was ever to make a list this would be somewhere at the top. David was on medication for his condition. I, like most people, thought that he was just a bad kid in need of a whoopin'. Maybe he did need that be he also needed someone to understand that thoughts were firing in his head that he hadn't learned how to control. It wasn't my job to teach him but if I was going to try to teach him I needed to understand where he was coming from first.

My mom

"If you want to see how a guy will treat you look at how he treats his mother."

This always seemed like terrible advice. First, finding a man that treats his mother well is not hard. Prisons, Klan rallies, and Internet comment sections are full of men that treat their mothers like royalty. Second, most of the men I know that adore their mothers treat women like Millennials treat music. What bothers me most about this saying is what it says about me. If I'm not mistaken it means that I will treat my lady with the amount of respect she deserves and nothing more. She won't get special treatment just because I've known her a long time.

If there is one thing I learned from TV it's that rich people and poor people treat their mothers completely different. If you grew up in a financially stable home you're predisposed to (at least while she's alive) hate your mother. You will duck her phone calls, write one woman/man plays about her, and share with your therapist how afraid you are of becoming her. If you grew up on the wrong side of the tracks you will write songs about her, tattoo her name on your body, and want to marry someone just like her. I've see both of these versions in action and they both seem equally ridiculous. I could never muster that much emotion for another human being that I wasn't having sex with.

My mother and I have had a pretty unfaltering relationship my whole life. I can only recall her throwing me under the bus one time. When I was in high school me, my mom and one of my teachers were having a talk and my teacher asked me why I hadn't gotten my permission slip signed for the school trip. I told her I forgot. My mother chimed in that I was just like my father, "always forgetting things". I replied that it "runs in the family" and we all had a good laugh. Later, in the retelling of this story to my father, my mother left out the part where she said he was forgetful. Instead she only referenced my hilarious zinger.

Understandably my dad took offence. He yelled at me for about 20 minutes about how hard he worked and how he had so many things to keep up with and that sometimes things slipped his mind. I totally understand how he could have felt disrespected by his son making fun of him in front of strangers. None of what he said bothered me. What bothered me was that he did this in front of my mother. I kept waiting for her to interject but she never did. Had she actually forgot that it was she who initially made the comment and that I just agreed? It wasn't like her to be this manipulative so I was really confused.

I'm proud to say that I didn't rat. This wasn't the first time I had been yelled at for no reason. It didn't happen often but when it did I just let my parents run out of steam. I felt bad that they were upset but it seemed like me pointing out that they were wrong would have just made things worse. I didn't feel betrayed by my mother. I was nonplussed. This wasn't the only time I felt like this around her.

…

I hadn't seen my brother Micheal for about 3 years. The first time I got to see him in all this time was in a courthouse where he was being sentenced to jail time. Micheal has been in and out of juvenile detention centers and jailhouses for a good part of his life. However, this was the first time I had ever been to a sentencing. The first time he went to juvie I was in school and I came home to learn that my brother was gone. Sometimes my mom talked about his first sentencing. She said, "they walked him though those doors and he never really came back." I remember visiting him and welling up with tears and not knowing why.

This day was nothing like that. I had grown used to his antics and to me this was just another thing we had to go through. I was a little shaken up when I realized that my mother didn't feel the same. Understandably, this was not something that she had gotten used to. Walking into the courthouse with her she seemed more confused than I had ever seen her. She couldn't find where the courtroom was and because I had never been there before I didn't know whom to ask. When we finally found the courtroom and the judge walked in and the bailiff asked us to rise she could barely stand. Seeing my brother walk in the room handcuffed was a sobering moment but not as sobering as the feeling of my mother's body leaning against me. At first I thought she needed me to move over because I was sitting too close. Thinking back I'm reminded of a scene in the TV show Arrested Development where Michael Bluth's mother Lucille uncharacteristically gives him a hug. Michael Bluth's response is "What's happening? Why are you squeezing me with your body?" I then realized that for the first time in my life that my mother was leaning on me. I wasn't there because I was the only person available. I was there because she needed me. I'm guessing that's what love feels like.

My Dad

One story my parents love to tell is about the day I was born. I was a breech birth, which means that I was born feet first. Had I pushed myself up I would have broken my spine, had I been pulled out I would have been strangled. To quote the Notorious B.I.G. the "umbilical cord's wrapped around my neck/ I'm seeing my death and I ain't even take my first step."

The doctor gave my father an ultimatum: save the mother or save the baby. This may be a little pompous of me but when I think about my dad's introduction into adulthood I think of this moment. Of course this wasn't his first tough decision. By the age of 29 he had survived the civil rights movement while living in the south, fought in a war, gotten married, and had two children. But this was something different. This was a decision that had the potential to directly change everything for him. For the record he chose my mom but that's beside the point. The point is that he made the decision.

...

If you subscribe to the 1950s model of fathering it all seems pretty simple. Dads are supposed to teach you how to do manly stuff. My dad taught me how to chop wood, tie a tie, mow a lawn, drive a car, fix a car, and drive a car even if you don't know how to fix it. I had to teach myself how to shave. Not because he couldn't teach me but because I didn't start shaving until I was 22. My dad also gave me the manliest lesson of all: my first lesson in homophobia.

It all started because as my sister was starting to gain weight. Because of this my mother decided to put her in a ballet class. I'm not sure how putting a pudgy teenage girl in a leotard will help her deal with her weight issues but I'll let it slide. For the record I too was gaining weight but I was never made to participate in physical activity. Again, I will let it slide.

Because my sister was in ballet my parents felt I needed an extracurricular activity. I don't remember if they ever asked me for my suggestions but they chose piano. I didn't object. Actually I was pretty excited about it. Because I was in the junior high marching band I already know how to read music and playing the piano was surely more practical than playing the sousaphone.

My first teacher was nice but apparently too expensive. I still remember the day I had to tell her that I wouldn't be coming back. She seemed to take it personally. I'm not sure why it was up to me to tell her this. This seemed like a job for an adult but my parents felt otherwise.

My next piano teacher was someone we knew from church. His name was Mr. Taylor. He didn't go to our church but he played piano at other churches and people around town knew who he was. I couldn't say definitively that Mr. Taylor was gay but it wouldn't be hard to imagine. Effeminate choir directors are in high supply in Black Baptist churches.

Once a week after school I would spend 30 minutes in Mr. Taylor's house learning the piano. This went on for about five weeks before my father rethought his decision. His explanation was that I was a quiet kid and he was afraid that if something happened I wouldn't tell him. I remember being offended. He seemed a little too flippant about the idea that someone would rape me and that would be that. I'm not sure if that was the right part of the argument to be upset about but it bothered me that my dad had already made this decision without my input. It wasn't like we ever had a discussion about what to do in case someone tried to corner me. He just assumed I wouldn't know what to do if the time came. I guess I should have been more offended that he assumed that Mr. Taylor was a rapist simply because he was (allegedly) gay.

I guess I didn't get upset about that part of the argument because the idea seems so ludicrous. The jump from homosexual to rapist seems like a pretty big leap. In the environment I grew up in the idea of a gay pedophile was pretty common but for some reason the idea never stuck with me. I didn't have openly gay friends. There were no positive portraits of gay people in movies or TV. Most of the music I listened to denounced it outright. But for some reason I never took the gay pedophile idea seriously. It's like when people say they wish everyone would be truthful and straightforward about everything. On the surface they may believe that but if they thought about it for a few minutes they would realize that no one wants to live in that world. I was a little saddened that my dad was one of those people that took the gay pedophile theory to heart but not altogether surprised. I will say one thing: if it weren't for gay people I'd know how to play piano right now.

…

I don't know much about cars, at least not on purpose. What I do know about cars I learned from driving crappy ones. A great deal of my teenage and early 20s was spent trying to keep my car from exploding. A great deal of that time was also spent helping my dad fix his cars.

One time we went to the junkyard to find a new alternator. I had seen them on TV but this was my first trip to a real life junkyard. There was no snarling canine protecting the precious metals. There was no toothless redneck trying to keep kids from stealing parts. There were no striped cars stacked a mile high waiting for their destruction. There was just a guy that sat at the front gate that charged people for the parts and what seemed like a never-ending maze of dead cars arraigned by make and model.

We walked for what seemed like miles before we reached what we were looking for. My father pulled out his tools and began dismantling the engine to salvage the alternator. When we finally got back to the front desk the guy apparently asked my dad for too much for the part. I was tired of walking in the sun and if it had been left up to me I would have just thrown the thing under the hood of a random car and called it a day. This was not my dad's approach. If someone else needed the alternator for this model car they wouldn't be able to find it if it's in the wrong car or the wrong place. We walked all the way back to the car where my dad pulled out his tools again and began reattaching the alternator. While reattaching the alternator my dad realized that what he actually needed was the voltage regulator, a much smaller part that costs much less. My dad probably doesn't remember this story but I will forever remember it as the time my dad taught me that if you're going to do something, do it the right way.

Big Brother #1

To me, my oldest brother Jermon (Jer-mōn) has always been an adult. Not just because he's 7 years older than me but because he's always carried himself that way. He loves telling me stories about how he used to babysit me and change my diapers. I never understood why a seven year old was in charge of a baby but it's his story so he gets to tell it however he wants.

He would always take me places with him because he knew I wouldn't rat him out if he did anything questionable. My sister on the other hand is a world-class snitch and my brother Micheal is typically more trouble than he's worth. So if he was going to go with any of his siblings it was going to be me. My first memories of being in a shopping mall are with him and his friends.

My brothers' early maturation really came into play when my family moved from Virginia to Texas. My parents' only mode of transportation was a moving truck that only had room for 4 people. In a 6 person family 2 of us would have to find our own way. Looking back it seems the smartest thing to do was for one of my parents (probably my dad) to drive the moving truck and for the other parent to take the bus with one of the kids. They decided instead to have Jermon and me take a Greyhound bus. So, in 1989 a 16-year-old boy got on a bus with his 9-year-old brother for a day and a half trip to Texas. I wish I could say that it was like the classic road movie where two brothers bonded over the open road but that was never our dynamic. Having Jermon around was always like having a third parent or at best a young uncle.

After his first year of college when I was about 13 he asked if I wanted to stay with him for a few days on campus at Texas A & M University. I went to class with him during the day and he laughed at me when I referred to his morning class as "first period". In the evenings when he had to go to work, he had one of his lady friends babysit me while I watched R rated movies. These random girls where always more than willing to oblige.

If I had to, I would defiantly cast a vote for myself as the more hansom brother but the one thing I always lacked was his confidence. Years later when I was in college I could never have convinced a beautiful girl into spending time with me let alone my younger sibling.

One day a girl took me to a comic book signing. I might have had a few Christian comic books that my mom bought for me but I'm pretty sure I never sincerely showed any real interest in comic books. Yet, here I was, standing in line with this gorgeous college girl at a comic book store in College Station, TX. I don't remember who was at the signing but it's totally possible that I was the proud owner of an autographed copy of The Amazing Spider-Man signed by Stan Lee before I threw it away years later.

It was a fun couple of days but in the end that was all they were, just a couple of days. Jermon and I did a lot of things together before I turned 18 but the one thing we never did was bond. My brother is like a politician in a lot of ways. He is always gregarious and amiable and when he talks you feel as though you're the only person in the room. However, you usually get the feeling that as soon as he goes to shake the next persons hand he's forgotten everything you've said.

I'll admit that for a while I wanted his approval more so than any other persons'. There defiantly was a time when I wanted to dress like him and have people say nice things about me like they did him. And I wanted to have birthday parties that filled my parents' house like he did. But I realized pretty early on that we are two completely different people who happened to be brothers that don't mind each other's company and I'm fine with that.

...

I was 21 years old when I discovered that Jermon was my half-brother. My siblings and I always suspected this but we never talked about it openly. The explanation that his name was a combination of my parents' names (Joe + Ramona) always seemed a little suspect. This didn't change my relationship with my brother or my mother. To me this information was further proof that no one knows what he or she is doing with their lives.

This did make me feel a little different about my father though. For him I had equal amounts of admiration and disappointment. He loved my mom so much that he decided to marry a woman that was pregnant with someone else's child. I knew exactly what it was like to love someone so much that I would be willing to do that. I also knew that had I gone through with those actions it would have been the biggest regret of my life. "Love makes you do stupid things" can be interpreted in so many ways and I was baffled by all of them.

The only thing that changed my relationship with my brother was me getting older. Before, our relationship had been student and teacher. Somewhere in my thirties it became apparent that he saw me as an adult. Now we're two adults that see each other sporadically and struggle to find common ground during conversations. If that's not brotherhood I don't know what is. Seriously, I'm not sure what it is.

Big Brother #2

The common bond my brother Micheal and I have is music. Most of my hip-hop knowledge came from our lengthy discussions on the 1985 Def Jam roster. When I tried to have these lengthy discussions with my classmates they feigned interest like a husband asking his wife how her day was. They didn't care that Scarface, Willie D and Bushwick Bill weren't the original Geto Boys, or that Rakim played the saxophone in high school. Sure, everyone around me listened to hip-hop but to them it was just music. You played it in your car so people thought you were cool and you played it at parties to get girls/boys to dance with you. To them it was a means to an end. To Micheal and me walking to the record store every Tuesday *was* the end. Unwrapping a band new cassette and reading the liner notes is the most legal fun a person can have.

Aside from our love of music there is only one other thing that we have in common: our face. Even though Micheal is 6 years older than me I've always been told that we look alike. (Personally, I don't see it.) There have been one or two occasions that while in the same room we were mistaken for twins. And when we're not in the same room people mistake me for him. I'm almost certain that no one has ever mistaken him for me. This is partly because Micheal has a personality that people remember for better or worse but also because no one ever remembers me at all.

This may explain why I've never seen him as a big brother. We've always been peers. Other than when we had to work for my grandfather chopping wood, I don't recall a time where it seemed he knew better than I did. If I learned anything from him it was what not to do.

Even if I didn't know him I would never consider Micheal a bad guy. He's just a guy that consistently makes the wrong decision. Decisions that have gotten him fired from countless jobs, decisions that have landed him in jail, and decisions that have hitched him to the wrong woman.

The combined factors of our likeness and his poor decision making skills were instrumental in me wanting to leave our hometown. My mother often worried that I would get arrested by mistake. Most of all I just needed to live in a place where I wasn't just "Micheals' brother." This is something that kids with charismatic older siblings deal with all the time. (Reggie Miller knows what I'm talking about.) I'm not sure how to say this without sounding cruel but I'm not sure I ever really respected him. Sure, I respected him as a human being that deserves a warm bed and a hot meal but not as a big brother who deserves my admiration.

That sounds really mean so let me see if I can put it another way. I've only watched one episode of Friends so I'm pretty sure I'm remembering this correctly. There is an episode where Monica (Courtney Cox) is talking about a sign that her brother Ross (David Schwimmer) made up when they were kids. The sign was him banging the inside of his fist together in front of his face. This was his way of giving the finger to their parents without actually having to give it. Monica goes on to say that she cried the night that he first made up the sign because she realized for the first time that she was cooler than her big brother.

I remember countless times when the neighborhood kids would challenge us to bike races or basketball games and I would watch Micheal confidently loose every time. By the way, the neighborhood kids I'm speaking of where my age not his. This is potentially another reason why I never really saw him as a big brother. I never played against him but I realized after a while that having him on my side was a detriment. Regardless, as long as I have a choice in the matter he'll always be on my team.

Little sister

Without question I am closest to my sister Joi. (My parents love misspelled names. I'm named after my grandfather Herman however they chose to spell it Hermon and pronounce it Her-'mon with the accent on the second syllable.) If Jermon helped me appreciate discipline and order and Micheal help shape my love of music then my sister helped develop my sense of humor. She was the first person to ever "get" me. Growing up most people saw me as either shy or pensive. She was the only one I trusted to understand my non-sequiturs.

That may be because we were alone a lot of the time. Are parents worked constantly and our older siblings where out doing whatever they were doing. The term "latchkey kid" always seemed sordid to be but I guess that is what we were. No one I knew came home from school to be greeted by their parents. In my day this is what we called "white people shit." Due to the sophistication of today's children this is probably now called "rich people shit" but you get the idea.

If we tried hard enough we could probably find recordings of our homemade radio shows and commercials. I remember one commercial for a game called "Knuckle Pee; It's the same as Pinochle except you hold out your knuckles and pee on them!" For the record we never played this game, only endorsed it.

We also enjoyed yelling out the window at strangers. When we were kids there was a Pepto Bismol commercial in which an Asian family explained how much they loved American food. My sister and I would take turns yelling "Hotdog" & "Pizza" out the window in stereotypic Asian accents. In our defense we were around 6 years old and didn't know what a stereotype, accent, or an Asian was. I have no defense for yelling out the window at strangers.

The first fight I ever got into was because I was defending my sister. She came over to me and told me someone was messing with her. So I rammed my Big Wheel into him. That was the first and last hit I got in. He pinned me to the ground and wailed on me for what seemed like an hour while all the neighborhood kids looked on. Eventually a girl that used to babysit me pulled him off. A few days later I was friends with the kid that beat me up as though nothing happened. My sister never fully explained what he did to her.

This was a mere foreshadowing of what was to come when my sister discovered boys. My first sense of this was years later when I was registering for college courses for the first time. My sister had gone with my mother when my mother registered for classes so my sister knew more about it than me. My mother thought it would be a good idea if she tagged along. We were together for about ten minutes before she disappeared and I was left standing in lines for hours trying to figure out how to get financial aid. It turned out that she had locked eyes with a boy she knew from somewhere and left me for dead. Although I was a little frustrated I understood that in the grand scheme of things this wasn't a big deal but I was still a little hurt by it. Especially when this started to be the rule rather than the exception.

Throughout our adolescence romantic partnerships didn't factor too much into our daily lives. The only place we were social was at our private Christian school and church. In both places the pickings were slim. Because my sister had not attended a public school since she was in elementary my parents decided to let her attend a public school for her senior year. For all of her life my sister was shielded from the reality of public school and she came out the other end a little worse for wear. Everyone else her age had 12 years of schooling to learn firsthand that girls could be mean, boys could be scum and high school could feel both crowded and lonely. She had a lot of catching up to do.

Shortly after she graduated she moved to the big city (Dallas, TX) and the oversimplified version of events is that she was seduced by the bright lights. The truth is I don't really know the more detailed version of events. After I left town I was too caught up fighting my own battles to help her fight hers. Somewhere in our early twenties we diverged and haven't been on the same track since. When we get back together we revert to our seven year old selves because that's all we know if each other.

...

My mother once asked me if I would ever consider moving back to Texas. Against my better judgment I told her that there was no reason for me to move back. She looked away and said quietly to herself "What about your family?" I decided not to answer that question because the truth is that proximity to my family would be pretty far down on the list of things that would make we want to relocate.

Like all people, the family I was born into had a lot to do with the adult I would eventually become. I place equal amount of responsibility for who I would become on the fact that I left my family where they were. Not having anyone to fall back on made me have to make my own decisions and more importantly I had to trust in those decisions.

What makes your family different from anyone else you will ever meet is that you can't hide from them. To a stranger you are a blank slate that needs to be filled in with details. Details about who you are and what you like. Details about what you've overcome. Details that can be as true or as false as you want them to be. You can't hide from your family. They know that when you were 12 your mom caught you wearing her bra. They know that the scene from Class of Nuke 'Em

High where the guy punches the other guy in the mouth and his fist goes down the other guys throat terrified you so much that you ran out of a crowded room screaming while the other kids laughed.

To some people that level of familiarity is the safety blanket they need to blossom into productive members of society. I am not one of those people. That level of familiarity would have only stunted my growth and make me second-guess every decision I made. My decision to leave my hometown had nothing to do with my family and everything to do with the fact that I needed space to become whatever it was I going to become.

Other things at which I've failed

1. Being able to play the Bob's Burgers theme song on the ukulele

2. Finishing Gabriel Garcia Marquez's *One Hundred Years of Solitude*

3. Learning Spanish before learning Vietnamese

4. Learning Vietnamese

5. Inviting my parents to my wedding

6. Getting into a PhD. Program

7. Having a dream job

8. Figuring out what to do with an artichoke

9. Working with Harris Wittels

10. Looking at my Facebook feed for more than 2 minutes before being disappointed in ever acquaintance I've ever had

11. Enjoying anything Bill Cosby related after 2015

12. Caring about anything on the cover of the magazines in the checkout line at the grocery store

13. Quitting masturbation

14. Finding a good reason to pay attention to Kanye West after 2010

15. Finding a porn site that doesn't separate people by ethnicity

16. Buying a car that I still wanted to drive after 10,000 miles

17. Anal sex

18. Landing a kick flip

19. Figuring out if my apartment complex really recycles anything we put in the recycling bin

20. Having a successful interaction with a woman at a night club

21. Watching The War starring Kevin Costner and Elijah Wood without tearing up

22. Figuring out why no one else has seen or likes The War

23. Understanding why fish sauce exist

24. Understanding the appeal of Keanu Reaves

25. Articulating an ambiguously racist thing that happened to me to a White person without them negating my experience

26. Being excited about my smartphone 24 hours after I've bought it

27. Beating a videogame

28. Mastering social media

29. Not getting angry when someone tells me to smile

30. Viewing owning an animal as something other than an unnecessary chore

31. Enjoying a Wes Anderson movie (I've seen them all)

32. Peeing with an erection and hitting the bowl.

33. Winning a fistfight

Conclusion (Heads)

You may be thinking to yourself "Lee, how can I too lead such an unsuccessful existence as the one you've lead all these years?" Well the answer is simple: I waited until the last possible moment to become interested in my own life. For the first 20 or so years of my life I lived in the most literal sense of the word. I breathed, slept and ate. I only dreamed when I went to sleep and that was by default. I didn't chase anything. Not even if I was late for the bus. I just figured another one would come and most of the time I was right. When I wasn't right I walked because I always accepted what was handed to me. Sometimes that's what you need to do. The Greatest Generation didn't get that name by blogging their complains during the Depression. But sometimes just accepting what's handed to you can lead to you discounting the world around you; like kids that grow up gangbanging on the North and/or East side of Long Beach, CA that have never actually been to the beach.

A lot of my childhood was me keeping my head down and getting through it. At any moment everything could fall apart so my only goal was to get to the finish line. The problem with living your life that way is that the only real finish line is death. By the time you get there it's too late. But even if you life your life just trying to get to the next day eventually you'll be too old to have anything but regrets.

Some people like to say, "it's never too late." Some people also like to say "LOL" in conversation instead of laughing. Neither one of these things is something you should say in real life. (Side note: my dad is one of those people that thinks LOL stands for "lots of love". The day he texted me that he was proud of me it felt very sarcastic.) If you're 30 years old and you want to join the Olympic gymnastics team in the next summer Olympics even though you've never done a backflip it's too late. Go to the Y, roll around on the tumbling mat and call it a day.

I spent my whole life waiting for something to happen. Throughout my entire adolescence I was completely aimless.

Every decision I made was for self-preservation and not much else. I did just enough to get me to the next level. Even when I got older and started pursuing things like audio engineering or writing I never went after it in the pursuit of being the best. It was just something I wanted to do, so I did it. And even while I was pursuing those goals I still always fell back on whatever gave me the most security. This usually meant that I would take an extra shift at a terrible job instead of chasing my dreams.

Even calling them "dreams" seems grandiose. They were really just things I wanted to do. I never dreamed because I had never been taught to. I don't blame anyone for this. When you grow up in an environment where everyone is just trying to survive you never really look at the bigger picture. If you don't want to be a musician or play sports there's not much advice to be had. Not a lot of people have made it out the hood by becoming biostatisticians. And you can't dream about becoming a biostatistician if you never knew they existed.

So in conclusion if you want to live like I did ping ponging through life then don't make a plan.

Conclusion (Tails)

You may be thinking to yourself "Lee, how can I too lead such a meandering existence as the one you've lead all these years?" Well the answer is simple: I never had a plan. I took everything that life threw at me and tried to make it work. The great thing about constant failure is that you get to do it in private. You can fly under the radar and you can try whatever you want: no one expects anything from you. Just remember that the moment you're successful everyone gets to wait to see you fail.

When I moved out when I was 19 I thought I knew what it meant to be an adult. I thought it meant that I was supposed to do everything on my own. I tried that and at the ripe age of 21 I had a nervous breakdown that lead to me dropping out of school. Without the breakdown I never would have dropped out of college and moved to Florida to be a recording engineer. Without my studying in Florida I never would have gotten my internship in Los Angeles. Without my firing from my internship I never would have gotten a "real job". Without my firing from my "real job" I never would have had the realization that I needed a career.

This all lead to me going back to school and getting the degree I set out to get when I was 19. It took almost a decade for me to become an adult. And I tried a lot of things before that happened. I wasn't particularly successful at any of the things I tried but I never cared for success as much as I cared about the experience. To be able to say that I once shared a pizza with The Bangles (the Rock band not the football team) or that I once saw a man walk out of a convenience store leaving a trail of blood behind him that no one seemed to notice is worth more than success to me. Some people have never experienced anything other than school, work and parenthood. Some people have never left their hometown or been yelled at by Alec Baldwin. (OK, most people have been yelled at by Alec Baldwin.) I'm not saying these people are failures. I'm just saying that they probably couldn't write a compelling autobiography.

And that's the thing about success and failure: there are no easy definitions. It's easy to think of success as this thing that lives outside of you but the truth is success is completely up to you. If you miss your target, regroup and pick another target.

…

When I turned 29 I looked in the mirror and saw a spare tire starting to grow. I flashed back to when I was a pudgy 13 year old and started working out the next day. I had never actually exercised on purpose so it was slow going at first. I did remember a few things that Jermon taught me about running. Once every few years I would go running with him. One year he invited me, my dad and Micheal to run a 5K with him. (Of course Jermon ran the 10K.) I managed to run the whole thing but at the end I swore to god and anyone who would listen that I would never run again. Now here I was 16 years later on a treadmill trying to lose weight. My vanity had finally trumped my laziness. I didn't even have proper running shoes. After my second workout my feet felt like they had been beaten with a hot bamboo shoot.

Eventually I got the hang of it and I added weightlifting to the mix. I eventually began to feel good about my regiment. I never enjoyed working out but I liked the results. I didn't walk around feeling stronger or faster but I did feel that if I needed to run half a block to push a child out of the way of a moving car I probably could without having to catch my breath halfway there. That was good enough for me. I also had more stamina during sex, which is probably a more useful scenario than the way I just mentioned.

Like all guys do I eventually started to wonder what I would look like with a six-pack. I took to the Internet to figure out what I needed to do. Most people think that you get a six-pack by doing millions of stomach crunches. True, crunches will help build you abdominal muscles but they won't get rid of the layer of fat that covers them. To do that you need to diet. I did what the Internet told me to do for about two months with no significant change in my physique. I decided to pull back and readjust my goal.

There is a picture of my brother Jermon that my parents still keep on their dresser. It's of him posing in his track uniform lying on the ground flashing a 100-watt smile. He was 16 in that picture and looked every inch a track star. He could easily take that picture today and look exactly the same. For 20 consecutive years and counting he's received a perfect score on his Army Fitness Test. If his Facebook statuses are to be believed he spends every day in the gym. This has been going on for over 40 years. Their will never come a day when he will look at himself in the mirror and say, "OK, I'm good." He'll never be finished. And that's totally fine because he knows he'll never be finished and he's accepted that.

My goals for my body are the same as Kevin Spacey's character in American Beauty "I just want to look good naked." I don't need rippling muscles. I just want to be able to eat ice cream, drink beer and still be able to run a 5K if I wanted to and I also want to be able to see my dick without sucking in my stomach. What I'm trying to say is that it's important to set goals in everything you do but it's even more important to admit to yourself that it will never be enough.

...

As kids we latch on to things that we love and try to suck them dry. As a teenager I loved music. One time I got into a fight with Micheal over music. Somehow we both ended up buying the same Arrested Development cassette. (That's Arrested Development the early 90s hip-hop group not the early '00s TV show.) He lost his copy and now he was playing mine. I ordered him to give it back. We got into a fight and he ended up breaking the cassette with his bare hands and smashing it into the ground under his heal. I cried actual tears. I was 14 years old. I cried because I would never hear Zingalamadui again. Over 20 years later you couldn't pay me to listen to Zingalamadui again. OK I'd listen to it if you paid me but I certainly wouldn't cry tears if you told me I would have to wait another 20 years to hear it again. But in that moment in time I loved music so much that I wanted to hear every song, read every article and watch every video that could fill my head. It took years to realize that even if I could hear every song every recorded it would never be enough. No comedian will ever get enough laughs, no actor will ever get enough awards, no athlete will ever get enough wins unless they define what "enough" means. After you do that you have to figure out if any of that stuff matters. So, you know, good luck with that.

Things I've learned

1. I used to think that being an adult meant doing everything yourself. It took a lot of knocks on the head to realize that it's ok to ask for help and it's even more important to accept it when it's offered.

2. I thought at 30 I would be too old for acne and too young for thinning hair. Wrong on both accounts.

3. Figuring out your purpose in life is one of the hardest things you will ever to do but it's even harder to accept it.

4. When cooking, clean as you go.

5. I stopped eating red meat and pork when I was 21. I did it because there were things I wanted to understand but I couldn't so I wanted to clear my mind and in doing so I decided to clear out my body. I'm not saying that you should stop eating meat. What I'm saying is that if

you're trying to reach enlightenment, do whatever it takes.

6. I have 3 siblings. All of us were spanked at some time in our upbringing. I don't think we came out any better because of it.

7. I was in a statistics class and on the last day my professor decided to show the "Statz Rappers" video (Google it). Because it parodies Nelly's "Grillz" video and because some people hadn't seen it he had to show it first so we could see the "Statz" video in context. We only watched the first 30 seconds but in those 30 seconds were every rap music video cliché you could think of. At first I was embarrassed that even though my people have done great things in this country this is more or less what we're known for. Then I felt ashamed of myself for feeling that I have to constantly prove myself to a majority that may or may not think I'm "less than." Then I felt angry at the people

who ever made me feel like I was "less than." Then I held my head up.

8. Life is sometimes unfair but sometimes it isn't.

9. When people talk about love and they say stuff like "when you've met that special someone, you just know." They aren't being coy. It's true. There really aren't any words for it.

10. If what you're cleaning with has ammonia in it, it'll work. At the very least it'll smell like it worked.

11. You're favorite album probably came out when you were a teenager. The older you get the harder it is to impress you.

12. No one likes being labeled. That's why when you ask someone what type of music they listen to he or she will inevitably say "everything." And then you ask them if they like country and then they say "no" and then they start naming the most obscure music they can think of. That is unless they *do* like country. In that case there's

no reason to ask them what they listen to. If a person listens to mostly country, you'll know.

13. Depression doesn't feel like you think it would. You think you'll feel sad but really you just feel exhausted and numb.

14. Sometimes your best isn't good enough but sometimes it is. When it isn't try to learn what you did wrong and try again. When it is be grateful and teach someone else what you did. That's all anyone who has ever been successful at anything has ever done.

15. It's extremely important to know who you are and to never confuse that with what your goals or talents are because if your goals fall out of reach or you lose your talent you won't have anything left.

16. One of the most refreshing things in the world is being able to look at a beautiful woman and seeing nothing but a beautiful woman. Not a conquest, not a tease, not a temptation, not a test. You're not worried about what she thinks about you because it really doesn't matter.

Even if you are talking to her, there's no ulterior motive. This feeling frees up a lot of headspace. (I assume the feeling is the same for a beautiful man.)

17. I spend a lot of my day trying to not be like the people that annoy me. Some days I am more successful than others. So if someone cuts you off in traffic or doesn't say "thank you" when you hold the door for them or doesn't pick up after themselves in the break-room give them a break, maybe they're just having an unsuccessful day.

18. 2 things that people will always find funny: 1) other people hurting themselves, specifically a person falling or a man getting hit in the balls. and 2) fish out of water (ex. old people doing young people stuff, animals doing human stuff, city folk going country)

19. The proper way to shave your face: 1) Exfoliate to get rid of dead skin, dirt and debris but no more than 3 times a week. 2) Lubricate with a pre-shave oil. It softens the beard. 3) Use a shaving brush when

lathering your face. It raises the hairs on your face and makes for a closer shave. 3) Shave in the direction your hair grows. Going against the grain can cause razor bumps. 4) Moisturize. Bonus: Invest in an alum block for any cuts you may get. I assume this works on any part of your body.

20. I used to be pretentious when it came to relationships. I thought I was above all the corny stuff they tell you on TV and movies but there's just as much truth in "Everybody Loves Raymond" as there is anywhere else.

21. One of the most fascinating/scary things about human beings is that we can rationalize anything: genocide, torture, paying $300 for a t-shirt, etc.

22. As far as I can tell there are three things you need to be successful: talent, persistence, and luck. Any amount of time spent dissecting pop culture will tell you that not only do you not need an equal amount of all these things, you really don't even need all three.

23. They say it's wiser to learn from other peoples mistakes but you learn so much better when your do it yourself.

Printed in Great Britain
by Amazon